MW01206610

COPING WITH

Choosing a Therapist: A Young

Person's Guide to Counseling

and Psychotherapy

Margaret E. Backman, Ph.D.

THE ROSEN PUBLISHING GROUP, INC./NEW YORK

Published in 1994 by The Rosen Publishing Group, Inc.
29 East 21st Street, New York, NY 10010

First Edition

Backman, Margaret E.
    Coping with choosing a therapist : a young person's guide to counseling and psychotherapy / Margaret E. Backman. — 1st ed.
        p.   cm.
    Includes bibliographical references and index.
    ISBN 0-8239-1699-5
    1. Adolescent psychotherapy—Juvenile literature.
    [1. Psychotherapy. 2. Emotional problems.] I. Title.
    RJ503.B33   1994
    616.89'0140024055—dc20   93-29661
                                                                        CIP
                                                                         AC

Manufactured in the United States of America

ABOUT THE AUTHOR ◇

Margaret Backman is a psychologist with advanced degrees in Clinical Psychology, Psychological Measurement, and Social Psychology from Columbia University and New York University. Her undergraduate studies were at The Pennsylvania State University and Barnard College, Columbia University.

Dr. Backman is currently a member of the mental health staff at the Office of Student Health Services of Barnard College. She is also on the faculty of the New York University Medical School and has a private psychotherapy practice in New York City.

Contents

Introduction

If you have picked up this book, you've probably been thinking about talking to someone about something that's bothering you. You may be having difficulties with school, or with friends, or with your family. Maybe you are upset about something, or you're feeling down or feeling bad about yourself.

In my years of experience as a psychologist I have listened to many people complain about their teenage years. They felt so unhappy. They didn't have anyone to help them with their problems. They had no idea how to go about getting help. In fact, some even thought that talking about their problems might make them worse. Others thought that being unable to handle their problems meant that they were weak. So they went on into their adult years still struggling with the same issues, not getting the kind of help that could have made their growing-up years so much better.

Of course, you could talk to a close friend or a parent about your problems. Sometimes a teacher or minister can offer advice. But sometimes you're not sure you want anyone close to you to know what is bothering you. You may feel ashamed, or afraid you'll get into trouble or get someone else into trouble. Maybe you're not even sure what the problem is: You've just been "moody" or you're not feeling right.

People may be telling you that you need to see some-one, that you should go for counseling or therapy. Maybe you've already been in individual or family therapy and you're not sure it really helped. Perhaps you resent being *made* to talk to someone you don't even know.

But what if *you* could find someone that *you* wanted to talk to? What if you could choose the therapist? "Sure," you may say to yourself, "that sounds good, . . . but I wouldn't even know how to go about it."

That's where this book comes in. It explains the different kinds of help that are available and the many professionals who are ready to help you. It also tells you how to go about finding a therapist who is qualified and experienced.

The book also includes some short "quizzes" designed to help you identify your upsetting feelings or thoughts and the problems you may be having in school, with friends, or with family. Your responses to these quizzes give you an idea of what you might need to talk to some-one about. In fact, you could take the quizzes with you when you first see the therapist so you have something to help you get started. The book also explains the process of therapy to make you feel more comfortable and to enable you to use therapy to your best advantage. After all, if it's your time and your life, why not get the most out of it?

CHAPTER 1

Does Talking about Problems Really Help?

Yes, for most people talking their problems over with someone really does help. It's interesting, this connection between talking and feeling better. No one really understands exactly how it works. Yet most people notice that when they share their problems and their feelings with others, they do start to feel better— and in many cases their lives change for the better too.

Sara and Jim

Sara had been dating Jim for over a year when he suggested that he needed "more space." He told her

1

2 ◇ COPING WITH CHOOSING A THERAPIST

that he still loved her but that he didn't want to see her every weekend. She had been feeling the same about him but had been afraid to say so. So she agreed to his idea.

Needless to say, she was devastated to learn that he had already been seeing someone else for the past month. She felt humiliated and betrayed. She didn't know whom to talk to. Her parents had never approved of Jim anyway, so they wouldn't give her any sympathy. She wanted him back. She wanted more space too, but she didn't want to lose him. Who could tell her what to do? She felt so depressed and angry. But how could she be angry with him? He had always been so nice to her.

No, she was angry with the other girl, she told herself. It was the other girl who had taken him away. She dreamed of hurting the other girl, of making a scene at her boyfriend's job, of begging him to come back and forgive her for the times she hadn't been nice to him. Sara eventually became so depressed that she felt she just had to talk to someone. Her two best friends were tired of listening to her. Whom could she trust? Who could help her?

Basil

No one ever took Basil seriously. Sometimes he played the class clown. At other times he could be a bully. Either way he was always getting into trouble. Now it was getting worse. Teachers picked on him for everything, he thought, even when he didn't do it. He wanted to break out of this bind.

But if he started trying to shape up, the other guys would get on his case and tease him. He had a reputation to live up to: being cool! He was getting tired of the role, but he couldn't see a way out of it. He needed to talk to someone, but to whom? He certainly couldn't talk to his friends. And his parents? Forget it.

Sara's and Basil's problems are not unusual. Yet everyone's situation is different, even though they may seem similar. How something is experienced depends upon the person and what that person brings to the situation. Both Sara and Basil feel that something is not right. Both are very unhappy with the way their lives are going, and both have a sense that they want to change. But more important, both have come to a point where they don't want to have to deal with this alone. They want to share their feelings, their fears, their hurts. They want to talk to someone who can understand, someone who can make them feel understood and accepted; yes, accepted even when that person learns that they aren't perfect, that they may not always have done everything right. They feel they are going down and down and down. But what to do? Where to turn? Who can help?

YOU ARE NOT ALONE

Feeling lost and confused at times is natural. Everyone sometimes needs to reach out to others for help. At times it is friends and family; other times it is a teacher or another adult in the community; and at other times it is trained professionals. Allowing yourself to turn to others for guidance and support can be one of the most important decisions you will ever make.

Counseling and psychotherapy can take different forms, but essentially they are special kinds of treatments or interventions in which you learn to deal with various problems: emotional, behavioral, and interpersonal. The goal is to improve the quality of your life. People go into therapy for many reasons, but basically they feel that something in their behavior is getting in the way of their ability to be themselves and to live productively.

Counselors or therapists are professionals specially trained to guide you through this self-examination and self-understanding.

BUT WHY THERAPY?

As you read this book you will learn how psychotherapy and counseling can help you take control of your life by:

- making better decisions
- changing your behavior
- improving your interpersonal skills
- improving your emotional state
- changing or adapting aspects of your personality
- dealing with personal conflicts
- learning more about yourself.

Reducing Tension

When you finally tell someone about something that is bothering you, you may find yourself breathing a sigh of relief. All of a sudden a burden is lifted off your back. Telling someone else about your problems or your sad feelings can actually relieve tension. Just having someone to listen to you—without even giving advice—may be all you need. Feeling understood and reassured makes you feel that you can go on.

Gaining Understanding and Insight

When you try to work through the problems on your own, you may go over and over the same ideas and worries, never seeming to get anywhere. But when you actually try to put the words together coherently to tell someone else, you bring order to the situation and you begin to exert control over your life. Hearing yourself say what is bothering you can clarify the actual problem and lead you on the road to a solution.

Solving Your Problems

Sometimes we just want to talk about feelings in a general way. But at other times we may be bothered by a specific situation. Perhaps you think that a teacher at school always picks on you; maybe your father doesn't treat you right; maybe you want to go to college but can't figure out how to manage it. These are very concrete problems and not easy to solve. They need to be examined closely and all aspects of the situation understood, along with your needs and desires.

You need to understand how you would like the situation to be changed. The person you talk to can help you understand what is realistic, and then plans can be made for achieving the end result that you'd like. That may sound impossible now, but it is a process that you take a step at a time.

Finding Your Own Way

Don't be fooled into thinking that what you need is someone who can give you answers. Often what is best is someone who can help *you* to find the answers. If you don't experience the growth and learning yourself, it does not belong to you. If someone else tells you what to do and you automatically do it, you may not really gain the understanding, and you will miss the emotional growth that is necessary for you to move on in your life. When you learn how to handle situations in your own life and to understand and deal with your own emotions, you become a much stronger and more independent person.

MAKING THERAPY WORK

Be Motivated

Whether or not therapy will work for you depends in part on efforts you put into it yourself. You need to be motivated

  . . . to *want* to learn about yourself,
  . . . to *want* to understand some conflict,
  . . . to *want* to change,
  . . . to *want* to solve a problem.

Take Responsibility

For therapy to have any effect, you have to keep your appointments and go on a regular basis. Psychotherapy is both a relationship and a process.

Meet the Challenge

You have to be willing to do much of the work. The therapist is there only as your guide. Some of it will be a struggle, even emotionally painful. You have to want life to be better and different for you.

Be Actively Involved

Yes, talking can help. You have to be actively involved. That does not mean always trying to impress your therapist, but "real" talking: sharing with your therapist your innermost feelings and thoughts. Sitting in angry stony silence is a waste of *your* time. You will not be punishing the therapist or anyone else—just yourself.

THE NEW ADVENTURE

Whether you realize it or not, you have already taken a very important step, perhaps for you the first big step: You have picked up this book. It is the beginning of a process, a process that may change your life. You have begun to make choices and to take control. By picking up this book and reading this far, you have shown that you are thinking about sharing your feelings, about solving your problems, and about getting someone to help you.

I have called psychotherapy a process, but it is really more akin to an adventure. It is like a trip, a voyage that will lead you around and about, into strange areas. You will discover new feelings and have new experiences. It will not always be easy, and like any growth experience, you will not be the same afterward.

Like any new adventure, you may not be sure where you are going or how things will turn out. There will be risks. After all, much of this is unknown territory for you. There is a certain amount of uncertainty. You may be afraid and looking for excuses. You may start doubting, saying to yourself,

"Maybe things aren't really all that bad."

"I've gone this far on my own, so why change things now?"

You try to convince yourself that your problems aren't all that serious—or are they? Read on . . .

CHAPTER 2

How Do I Know If

I Really Need

Therapy?

I t's true that in life we all have problems, and not everyone goes to a therapist or counselor. But sometimes the problems are just too difficult to be shared with a friend or family member, or maybe you are too embarrassed or afraid to tell anyone you know. A third party who is not involved directly in your life can often give you a perspective that you can't get from those you know. In many cases the nature of the problem is such that someone with training is the best person to help you.

To help you answer the question, *"How do I know if I really need therapy?,"* I have included some quizzes or checklists describing typical problems or disturbing feelings that people bring to therapists. If you find yourself checking off several of the items, and particularly those marked with a star, you should seriously consider getting help from a professional. These self-quizzes are intended to get you thinking about what may be troubling you.

If you find that your bad feelings or problems have been very intense and going on for a long time, you should consider finding someone with training and experience to help you through this period.

USING THE SELF-QUIZZES

The self-quizzes or checklists are divided into four sections:

    I. School
   II. Friends and Relationships
  III. Family
  IV. Personal.

Take a piece of paper and for each section copy down the sentences that describe you. Beside each sentence write the number that indicates how intense or important the sentence is to you, using the scale below.

Give yourself:	If it is:
3	very much like you,
2	often like you,
1	sometimes like you,
0	not like you at all.

Later you'll be tallying up your scores to help you answer your question: "How do I know if I really need therapy?" The higher the score, the more intense your problems are, or the more problems you have. The self-quizzes are only a rough gage, and it is hoped they will serve to motivate you to seek help if need be.

PROBLEMS CHECKLIST

SECTION I.   SCHOOL

Seems like me:

very much	somewhat	hardly at all	not at all
3	2	1	1

_____ I hate school.

_____ I can't concentrate on my work.*

_____ I'm having trouble with my schoolwork.

_____ I keep cutting classes and missing school.

_____ I've just changed schools.

_____ I'm applying for college and feel confused and afraid.

_____ I'm graduating soon and am worried about my future.

_____ I'm always in trouble and I don't know why.

_____ Teachers always pick on me.

_____ I'm always being told that I can do much better. (But I don't know how; how do they expect me to do that?)

_____ Other _____

_____ Total score: School

SECTION II.   FRIENDS/RELATIONSHIPS

Seems like me:

very much	somewhat	hardly at all	not at all
3	2	1	1

_____ I have trouble making friends.

_____ I feel all alone.*

_____ I'm always getting into fights.

_____ Other kids always pick on me.

_____ I feel like an outsider.

_____ I think I'm in a bad crowd but don't know what to do.

_____ My boyfriend (or girlfriend) doesn't always treat me right.

_____ I've just broken up with my boyfriend (girlfriend).

_____ My boyfriend (girlfriend) wants to have sex and I'm not sure I do.

_____ I've been having sex and I feel confused and upset.

_____ Other _____

_____ Total score: Relationships

SECTION III. PARENTS AND FAMILY

Seems like me:

very much	somewhat	hardly at all	not at all
3	2	1	0

_____ I hate someone in my family.

_____ Someone in my home drinks too much.

_____ Someone in my family uses drugs.

_____ I'm always fighting with my mother or father.

_____ My parents fight a lot.

_____ I don't feel like I have any parents.

_____ I'm afraid my parents are going to get a divorce.

_____ My parents got divorced when I was young, and sometimes it still bothers me.

_____ My parents punish me too severely or without good reason.*

_____ My parents don't understand me.

_____ I miss my father (or mother).

_____ I hate my father (or mother).

_____ My family has moved to a new home.

_____ My father (or mother) died.

_____ I never see my father (or mother).

_____ I'm having problems with my brother or sister.

_____ I'm having problems with my stepbrother or stepsister.

_____ I resent my father's new wife or girlfriend.

_____ I resent my mother's husband or boyfriend.

_____ I'm worried about my grandfather (grandmother).

_____ I'm worried about my uncle (aunt).

_____ I'm worried about my cousin(s).

_____ I was adopted and I have some feelings about this.

_____ I don't feel like I have a home.

_____ I don't feel loved. *

_____ I lived for a while in a foster home.

_____ Someone in my family has touched me in a sexual way. *

_____ I may have been abused by a baby-sitter or other person. *

_____ Other _____

_____ Total score: Parents and Family

SECTION IV.   PERSONAL

Seems like me:

very much	somewhat	hardly at all	not at all
3	2	1	0

_____ I have no self confidence. *

_____ I'd like to change.

_____ I feel I am worthless and not likable. *
_____ I don't sleep very well.
_____ I cry a lot.
_____ I don't know who I am.
_____ I feel depressed.
_____ I feel anxious, afraid.
_____ I think I've been sexually abused. *
_____ I have been raped. *
_____ I think I might be gay and am concerned.
_____ I keep doing things over and over.
_____ I can't stop thinking about something.
_____ Something bad happened to me and I can't tell anyone. *
_____ I use drugs.
_____ I use alcohol.
_____ I've been throwing up a lot. *
_____ I eat very little.
_____ I binge.
_____ I cut myself when I'm upset. *
_____ I dress really freaky, but only pretend I'm cool.
_____ I have too many responsibilities.
_____ I think something bad happened to me when I was young. *
_____ I have a secret and can't tell anyone.
_____ Someone I know needs help. *
_____ I'm afraid I might be pregnant. *
_____ I think about killing myself. *
_____ Other _____

_____ Total score: Personal

TALLYING THE SCORES

Add up the total score for the four sections:

_____ School

_____ Relationships

_____ Parents and family

_____ Personal

_____

_____ Sum: Overall Score

Red Flags

- *Overall Score: 15 or more*

    If you get an overall score of 15 or more, you should speak to a professional who can help you deal with these problems.

- *Section total: 6 or more*

    If your total score on *any* of the sections adds up to 6 or more, that is another indicator that you should speak to someone who can help you.

- *Section total: 10 or more*

    If you've scored a 10 or more in any section, don't wait. Do yourself a favor and seek help right away. There are solutions.

These scores are only relative indicators. The higher the score, the more intense or the more problems you may have. If you get a lower score than indicated above, it doesn't necessarily mean that you can't benefit by talking to someone.

Individual Items

You should definitely seek professional help if you have marked any of the asterisked sentences, no matter what rating you gave them, or if you rated any of the sentences with a 3.

WHAT THE SCORES MEAN

Whether you should speak to a counselor or a therapist depends on the nature of the problem and other circumstances that are discussed later, particularly in Chapter 4. Solving school problems may be as simple as learning new study skills or different ways of behaving. On the other hand, your difficulties may be related to other issues that become more clear after you have completed the check lists.

Relationship problems can be very upsetting. They can affect how you feel about yourself and can sometimes make you act in ways that you later regret. The pent-up anger, depression, despair can become overwhelming, particularly when you don't know where or how to direct it. Also the frustration of knowing that something is not right, but not knowing what to do about it or how to behave or how to feel can be quite upsetting. The desire to be popular, to be accepted is important for many people at different stages of life, but it takes on particular importance in the teenage years. And certainly no one wants to feel rejected or unloved.

A good counselor or therapist can help you look at these confusing feelings. You can speak to this person about issues that you may be hesitant to discuss with your close friends or parents, such as sexual feelings or practices.

Again, a section total of 6 is a red light suggesting that you have some serious issues that need discussing. Each of these items can have a special meaning to you, so don't compare yourself to others, thinking that their situation is worse or that they have handled it differently. A therapist will help you deal with it in your own unique way.

Please seek out a therapist if even one sentence followed by an asterisk (*) applies to you. These instances can be very troubling but do not mean that you have done anything wrong. You may think that something that happened a long time ago can't be bothering you now. But in fact it can.

Some of the items in the self-quizzes have very serious consequences. You may try to ignore their impact or importance, but believe me, they can affect you deeply and in ways that you may not realize. Sometimes we repress things; that is, we don't let ourselves think about them, only to have them reappear in surprising ways, even years later. That is why some sentences are marked with an asterisk (*); they *should not be ignored.* Each and every item is very important. Think about each sentence no matter what number you gave it. Be as honest with yourself as you can be, and make the best decision you can about going for help.

WHEN NOT TO GO TO A THERAPIST

To give some balance to all of this, I do not mean to imply that every problem is best dealt with by psychotherapy or professional counseling. There are certainly problems that you can deal with by yourself. In fact, one of the goals of therapy is to help you learn how to handle things on your own. But another goal is to help you know *when* to go for help and how to get it when you need it.

Good friends, family, a teacher, a religious person (minister, priest, rabbi, nun) can often provide help. Sometimes just having someone listen to your problems is help enough. Sometimes these people can give you good counsel. And often if you really think about it yourself, you can reason out what is happening. Some of you who are well organized may even solve some of your dilemmas by making lists: the good and the bad sides of a decision you have to make, for example. Some of you may be very good at confronting people when you don't like what they are doing. Some of you may know how to be diplomatic or firm. And you may be comfortable with the way things are going, even though it's not always what you'd like.

Yes, there are the ups and downs, the broken relationships, the losses, and the struggles. This is part of life and one doesn't always have to go into psychotherapy to get through the rough roads. Friends, family, and other important people in your life can lend an ear, offer advice and counsel.

But the important thing to learn is when to go for help. That point is usually reached when you feel you can no longer cope on your own, when you feel others may be tired of listening to your problems, when you feel there is no one to talk to, when the problem is beginning to feel overwhelming or has been going on too long. Then someone else needs to get to know you, to understand you, and to help you. But therapy isn't for everyone . . .

When Is Therapy Not Effective?

Although therapy works most of the time, there may be situations in which it may not be too effective:

- If you are not motivated to go. This may happen because someone else is making you go, such as a parent or the school or the law.
- If you just don't like talking to others or are not

comfortable in relationships. (Yet for some, therapy becomes the beginning of learning how to have relationships with others.)

- If you don't like the therapist. There are people who call themselves therapists but are not well trained. But even among those who are well trained, the matter of personality is vital. You need to find someone with whom you personally are comfortable, with whom you can talk. That is why it is important to learn how to select a therapist (as discussed in Chapters 4, 9, and 10), and to be able to evaluate your progress and the therapy (as discussed in Chapter 11).

- If you don't have support from parents. For example, if your parents do not like the idea, they may ridicule you, refuse to pay, or try to get you to quit every time you show anger or don't behave just right. Many parents like to think that they should be the ones you turn to for help, and may not like your going outside the family for support. Not only may they fear being criticized for not having been good parents, but they may see it as a rejection of themselves.

- If you don't have support from your friends. Friends may be unsupportive because they don't realize how upset you are or what is troubling you. Or they themselves may be having problems and your admitting that you want to go for professional help may be threatening to them. So, out of ignorance or uneasiness, they may tease you. Your parents and your friends may also fear that you may criticize them in therapy.

- If therapy is not part of your cultural customs. In

some cultures going for therapy is just not done. That could make it difficult for you to participate as openly as may be necessary should you give therapy a try.

- If you hold back in therapy. If you feel that you cannot be open, you may be wasting your time. But be aware that it takes time to build up trust and to feel comfortable. If at first you are not sure whether you can be open, that is not a reason not to start. But if over time you cannot be open, you need to consider whether it will help you. Sometimes telling the therapist that you are having trouble talking about something is a way to move toward a difficult subject.

- If you are going into it to please others, and not for yourself.

- If you blame others for your condition and refuse to look at yourself.

- If you want someone to give you answers, rather than trying to work with someone to learn about yourself.

There may also be practical reasons for not seeing a therapist. You may not have the time because of school and other activities. You may live too far from a trained psychotherapist. Or the time may just not be right. You may need some distance from what is bothering you. Later in your life you may be in a better position to tackle your problems. Perhaps you will be in a better financial position or feel more independent and less accountable to others.

Make sure that these are not just excuses to put off something that might be better dealt with now. Therapy can be effective in spite of parents, friends, and cultural customs. Everyone who goes into therapy has some resistances, some ambivalence about it. These resistances are discussed in the next chapter.

CHAPTER 3

Sometimes I Feel Like Talking to Someone, But . . .

. . . I CAN HANDLE THIS MYSELF

You may have been dealing with this problem for a long time, and when you get cold feet about talking it over with a professional, you tell yourself, "Well, I've been handling it all along by myself and I've managed so far." But have you? Are things starting to get out of control? Could things be better? Have you really tried everything you might? Are you denying to yourself just how bad things have become?

...I *SHOULD* BE ABLE TO HANDLE THIS MYSELF

The difference between this response and the one above is the word *should*. You may see it as a sign of weakness that you are looking for help, that you haven't done enough, or that you are giving in or giving up. What you fail to realize is that knowing when and where to go for help is actually a sign of strength. Knowing how to get help shows good sense.

Business executives, for example, always have consultants of one kind or another, so why not you? Find someone who will help you think through and analyze what is bothering you. The word *should* is like an inner voice that nags at you, that makes you feel guilty. Perhaps it is not your voice but another voice: your father's or your mother's voice perhaps? But often instead of helping you find a solution, the word *should* stands in your way and prevents you from reaching out when help is available and necessary.

...I'M TIRED OF ADULTS TELLING ME WHAT TO DO

"It's bad enough having my parents tell me what to do," you may be thinking. "I don't need some other grown-up telling me what to do." That, of course, is a misconception about therapy. True, a counselor or therapist is an adult, but one who acts more as a guide helping you to find your way. If your parents or other adults are insisting that you go into therapy, you may feel resentful that they are trying to get you into line. Therapy will thus seem more like punishment, not something that helps you.

... I'M NOT SURE I CAN TRUST ANYBODY

Having been let down or betrayed by someone you trusted can make it hard to trust again. And particularly, it is hard to put your trust in someone you do not even know, as is the case when you begin therapy.

... I DON'T WANT TO BE DEPENDENT

Related to trust is a fear that once you become involved with people and begin to trust them you will become dependent. You may be concerned that once dependent, you will not be able to let go, to separate from this person, that the person will take control of your life. Although therapy involves both trust and dependency, the eventual goal is to help you learn how to take control of your life and become more independent. But before you jump right in to put your trust in a therapist, read later chapters to learn how to evaluate the therapist and understand what the process of therapy is about.

... I'M AFRAID OF WHAT OTHERS WILL THINK

You may be afraid that people will think something is wrong with you, that you are different. Some people may believe the myths about psychotherapy that abound in society. But you need not let other people's misinformation hold you back. In fact, once they see the changes in you, they may become interested in therapy themselves. People often judge something harshly when they are afraid of it, even though they secretly wonder if they could benefit from it themselves. Don't let others' opinions hold you back from your own growth.

...I KNOW MY PARENTS WON'T LIKE IT

The "others" you may be concerned about could be your parents. Depending upon their cultural background and their own experiences, they may not be supportive of your seeking psychological help. When you complain about not being able to do something or feeling bad, they may tell you that you just need to try harder, that you are letting things get the best of you. The concept of "depression" or "emotional problems" doesn't exist for them.

Sometimes parents feel that problems should stay within the family and be dealt with by the family, not outsiders. Should this be the case, you will need to have some other authority figure help you out, such as a teacher or the school counselor or school psychologist. Once they understand your needs, they can help you approach your parents or can intervene for you.

When parents finally understand how important it is for you to speak to a professional, they become supportive. Even in such cases, parents may feel guilty; they may think that you blame them for what is happening, or that they have not been good parents. They may be ashamed and worry what others in the community think of you and them. If these concerns exist in your family, speaking with your therapist or going to family therapy together can often help parents to become more accepting and more supportive.

RESISTANCE TO THERAPY

When you first think of going to therapy it may seem like a good idea, but as you come closer to looking for a therapist, making an appointment, or actually going to the first session—all of a sudden you start having reservations. This is natural, particularly if it is your first time. But even if it isn't the first time, you may be reluctant underneath.

In psychology we refer to this uneasiness about going into therapy as *resistance*. Some of the resistance is based on myths or ideas that are misleading. You may have heard them from family or friends or perhaps on TV. In part, the negative ideas may have a basis in reality. On the other hand, such negative thoughts may be used as excuses when you are feeling uncertain about taking the big step into finding help.

Debunking the Myths

Let's look at a few of these negative ideas or myths to see if we can reframe them into positive statements that will help you overcome your resistance. We call them myths, because they are ideas that have been passed down from generation to generation with little basis in fact, or they are essentially misleading in what they imply.

Myth #1. Talking with someone about your problems only makes them worse.

It's true that sometimes when you talk about your problems it stirs things up. But this is a necessary part of the healing process. Burying uncomfortable things does not mean that they go away. On the contrary, they lie inside gnawing at you, popping out when you least expect them or want them to.

Myth #1 Reframed: If I get things off my chest, I'll feel better.

Myth #2.   Going to a therapist means you are crazy.

What you may be afraid of is that the therapist will find out that you *are* crazy (whatever that word means to you). Some people who go into therapy do have serious mental disorders or illnesses. However, the vast majority of people who seek counseling and psychotherapy are trying to solve problems and deal with unpleasant feelings or situations. They hold down jobs, go to school, get married, and do all the usual things of life. Therapy just helps them do them better and move on.

Myth #2 Reframed: Going to a therapist means I am trying to help myself.

Myth #3.   No one can help me.

You may feel that way when you are overwhelmed or have not had people there for you in the past. Often the solution is just finding the right person to help you, someone comfortable who has the training and experience.

Also, you may have to change your definition of help. Don't expect the counselor or therapist to have immediate concrete answers for you. The process of therapy is for you to find the solutions and make the changes in your life. You will learn to help yourself.

Myth #3 Reframed: I'm going to take control and find someone who can help me.

Myth #4.   I'll find out something about myself that I'd rather not know.

You may also find out things about yourself that you like. People with low self-confidence often have trouble believing that they have strengths, good points. What you learn in therapy is how to make the best of what you have and how to modify and change the things that you don't like.

Myth #4 Reframed: It doesn't mean I'm a bad person, just because there are things about me that I don't like.

Each of these myths may have some element of truth. Some may apply to some people some of the time, but they certainly are not hard and fast rules. And as you can see from the reframing, they can be thought of in a more positive way that can help you fight through the resistance.

WHAT CAN I DO FOR A FRIEND WHO NEEDS HELP?

Barbara and Carmen

Carmen was very concerned about her friend Barbara. She knew that Barbara was very unhappy at home and didn't get along with her parents. The two girls used to talk a lot and try to support each other. But recently Carmen had come to realize that she was doing most of the listening and giving most of the support. She was beginning to resent this.

Barbara seemed interested only in her own problems and was getting more and more depressed. She cried a lot, she didn't pay any attention in school, she was late a lot because she just couldn't get out of bed. But what really worried Carmen was that Barbara had started talking about how life was not worth living, how she was just a burden and people would be better off without her.

Carmen tried to reassure Barbara that she liked her and that everything would turn out fine. But this only seemed to have a momentary effect. To make matters worse, Carmen didn't want to spend so much time with Barbara and found herself pulling away. Yet she felt guilty. She liked thinking of herself as someone others could turn to when they had problems. She didn't want to be one of those people who found Barbara a burden. At the same time, she was worried about her; all that talk about life not being worth living was scary. She couldn't even let herself think the words *kill herself* or *suicide*, but that was what she was afraid of.

Carmen didn't know what to do. She knew she couldn't tell Barbara's parents; they would never believe her, and might even punish Barbara. What if she told a teacher? Would Barbara get thrown out of school? Would they put her in the hospital? Would Barbara be mad at her, never speak to her again?

All these thoughts and fears ran through Carmen's mind. Then one day she was speaking to the school counselor about some tests she was to take, and she told the counselor that she was worried about her friend. At first, she didn't want to give Barbara's name, but after talking for a while she realized that she would have to identify her or there would be no way of helping her. The counselor explained that there were people available to talk to Barbara and to offer to help her with her family problems. It was too much for Carmen to shoulder. The counselor suggested that Carmen urge Barbara to come in to talk with her. Carmen could come along if that would make Barbara feel better.

Carmen saw her friend later that day. Barbara had black circles under her eyes, she was pale and thin. Carmen knew she had to speak. To her surprise, Barbara was not mad at her for talking to the counselor, but she did not readily agree to go for help either. Like many others, Barbara subscribed to the many myths that get in the way of seeking counseling or therapy. But Carmen explained that she could no longer listen to her friend's problems; it was too much responsibility for her, and she could no longer play "therapist." So Barbara gave in. Both girls went later that day to the counselor's office.

Carmen waited nearby to give her friend moral support. Her earlier reluctance had now turned to relief. Her worries about getting her friend into trouble seemed to fade as she realized that Barbara would have gotten herself into more trouble on her own.

The school counselor talked to Barbara for a long while. In the end she helped her to find a good therapist outside of school, whom Barbara continued to see for several months. After a while even her friends could see changes. Barbara's spirits were better; her face brightened, her school work improved, and she was handling problems with her parents better. Not everything was perfect; there were the down periods, but they were not so low and Barbara bounced back sooner. Carmen had helped her friend.

The story of Barbara and Carmen illustrates only one of the many ways that friends and relatives can intervene to assist someone in emotional distress. Listening to your friend's problems and being supportive can go a long way, but as we have seen, it is not always enough.

You should not feel that you have failed your friend because your support has not made things better. Nor should you feel guilty that you no longer like listening and trying to help. These feelings may be signs that you are not reaching your friend, that the problems are bigger than you can solve. Rather than seeing this as a sign of failure, see this instead as a warning light that something else needs to be done. You may need a new approach. A professional may need to be called in.

CHAPTER 4

Why Can't I Just Talk To My Family and Friends?

WHEN TO INVOLVE YOUR PARENTS

With some problems, you may be satisfied sharing them with a friend or someone in your family. With more serious problems, however, it is usually best to try to discuss them with your parents first. If they can't help you directly, they can direct you where to go for help.

You may be one of the fortunate people whose relationship with your parents allows you to go to them and tell them your problems. Maybe you have already done that, many times in fact, and have found them to be caring and wise. That's terrific.

Most parents do want to listen; they care and try to be understanding—more so than you may give them credit for. If you are under legal age, in many situations you must have your parents' permission before professionals are allowed to intervene. (This is so, except in situations such as physical or sexual abuse or possible physical harm to you or someone else.)

MY PARENTS CAN'T HELP ME . . .

In the ideal situation it is good to speak to your parents when you are struggling with a problem. I say "ideal," realizing that not all parents are able to give this kind of help.

Problem Areas

There may also be family situations that make it hard for you to bring up certain issues.

Problem #1.   Both of your parents may not be available to you. In this day and age many students are living in a home with only one parent. You may be hesitant to bring up certain issues with your parent, who already may seem overwhelmed. The other parent may not live nearby. Perhaps you haven't even seen that parent for a long time or ever.

Problem #2.   Your parents don't have the knowledge to give you the kind of advice or help that you need. You may feel that they will not understand.

Problem #3.   Your parents may have their own problems that may make it difficult for you to speak with them.

Problem #4.   Your parents' needs may be in conflict with your needs.

Robert

Robert had always been able to turn to his father for help, but after his parents got divorced, he felt deserted, all alone. When his mother started dating again, he was confused. At first he liked the idea of having a new "dad," someone who could show up at football games, someone he could tell his friends about. His own father had remarried and moved to another state. He hardly ever saw him now.

But from the first day he met Matt, his mother's new boyfriend, Robert found him cold and distant. And he particularly resented Matt's criticizing him in any way. After all, Matt wasn't his father; why should he have to listen to him? When his mother told him that Matt would be moving into their home with them, Robert felt the anger rising up inside him. But he didn't say anything.

As the days went on, Robert started staying out later and later. One night he didn't come home at all. He walked the streets, hung out with friends at the local bowling alley, and then slept in the back seat of a friend's car.

His mother was furious with him. When he tried to tell her how he felt about Matt, she told him that he would have to get used to it, that Matt was a good person and that they would learn to get along. But Robert felt it was more of an order, that she didn't really care how he felt. Robert needed someone to turn to. He didn't want to tell his friends; he didn't want them to know what was going on at home or to think he wasn't cool. He didn't want anyone to know that he was upset.

Robert needed to communicate with his mother, but his attempts were not effective. Part of the problem was that he tried to communicate mostly by acting out: staying out late, withdrawing at home, staying alone in his room without talking to anyone. His mother seemed set in her decision; nothing he could do or say would change her mind.

Robert's story did have a positive ending, although the road to it was rocky. What eventually happened was that Robert got picked up by the police after getting into a fight with a friend. This was the beginning of a series of run-ins with the law. A counselor at the police department had a chance to speak with him one evening. Robert broke down and confided in the counselor, telling him that he felt he had no home and was unloved.

The counselor got Robert's permission to speak to his mother. When she came to understand the seriousness of what was happening, she agreed to speak to a family therapist with Robert.

Robert didn't like the idea of seeing a therapist at first. He felt that he had been singled out as the bad one, that this was part of his punishment. But he noticed that after several sessions his mother was beginning to relent on her idea of having Matt move in so soon. Seeing that she cared enough to make such a decision, Robert began to feel less abandoned, less angry.

Matt did eventually move in, but not until Robert had gotten to know him better and feel more comfortable with him. His mother had allowed him to be part of the decision. The truth is that Robert never did grow close to Matt, but his resistance lessened as he felt more secure in his own home.

Robert's mother had learned to listen and to understand; so had Robert . . . and so had Matt, who also had to learn how to be part of the new family.

PROBLEMS IN COMMUNICATION

If you find that you can't speak to either your mother or father about what is bothering you, that in itself is a problem that may need to be addressed, a problem of communication and understanding and trust.

If you are having trouble communicating with your parents, another adult may be able to intervene and speak to them on your behalf, paving the way for you to speak to them.

If you do eventually go into therapy, your therapist will probably want to talk to your parents as well as to you. In fact, most therapists will not see the young person unless they also meet with at least one of the parents. Even if you are older, the therapist may want to meet with one of your parents once in a while, perhaps alone or in your presence.

FAMILIES FROM DIFFERENT CULTURES

If your parents were not born in this culture, they may have a different way of solving family problems. In some cultures family members are not expected to go outside the immediate family in discussing problems. Certain situations, such as those involving sex, mental illness, and failure in school, are considered shameful, worthy of severe punishment, and certainly not to be discussed outside the family.

Depression or anxiety also may be concepts that are not

part of your culture. You would be considered "lazy" or "weak" if you gave into those feelings. "Work harder," may be your parents' advice when you say you are overwhelmed by school. In their thinking, the way to get over stress is to tackle your problems, to do more!

Sue Won

Sue Won was having great trouble concentrating on her studies. She had been a good student in high school, but now in her first year of college she was having a hard time. Her grades did not satisfy her parents. She found herself lying and not telling them about her schoolwork.

In fact, Sue Won was finding it harder and harder just to sit down and do her work. She would avoid it, talking to her friends on the phone, going out at night with her new school friends. She had even taken to drinking beer, something she knew her mother would hate.

Sue Won knew that things were getting out of control. She also had a sense that she knew why. Last year she had learned that her father had been seeing another woman, and that he might even have another family with that woman. She wasn't sure, but she had overheard her parents arguing. She did know that her father was hardly ever home anymore, and that when he was home their only interaction was about her schoolwork and how she had to study harder.

Sue Won lost all her energy; she would sleep late in the morning, take naps in the afternoon. She felt sad and confused. When she was alone, she would think about that argument she had overheard. She imagined the other family, wondered who the other children were. Was her father happier with them?

She couldn't tell her mother what she had heard. It was not respectful for her to challenge or criticize her parents. She was obedient and respectful to them. But more and more when she talked to her mother, they got into arguments.

The day that Sue Won found out that she had failed the math exam, she was devastated. When she got home, she tried to look happy but she couldn't keep up the front. When her mother yelled at her for not keeping her hair neat, and not being nice to her brother, it was the last straw. Sue Won broke down and cried and cried. Her mother, not knowing what was going on, only scolded her more. Sue Won felt she couldn't tell her mother about the disgrace at school. Her mother would experience it as shame before the neighbors, the relatives.

An argument erupted around the kitchen table. Sue Won cried and her mother yelled. Not knowing what to do, Sue Won grabbed a large glass and smashed it over her arm. The glass cut her slightly, enough to cause some bleeding. She grabbed a piece of glass and acted as though she would cut her arm. Her brother and her mother, horrified, held her in her chair until she could calm down.

For the rest of the weekend there was tension in the family. All her mother would say to her was, "I can't believe you are my daughter." Sue Won didn't know how to win back her mother's respect, yet she didn't know where to go with her pain.

Without realizing it, she had acted out her pain and frustration to show everyone how desperate she was, how bad she was feeling. Yet she never told anyone what was bothering her. How were they to understand even a little bit if she wasn't able to express herself?

Sue Won later realized that her dramatic actions were a desperate cry for help. But people couldn't read her mind. Although she admitted that she didn't really want to hurt herself, once she had calmed down she could see that by accident she could have caused harm. Glass could have cut a vein or an artery, she could have damaged her eyes. She could have hurt others in the room.

She knew that she would have to learn other ways to express her frustration and anger, to bridge the cultural gap. This way only created greater stress in the family. Sue Won eventually confided some of her problems to a teacher that she liked. The teacher in turn suggested that Sue Won talk to a counselor in the college's mental health unit.

Working with the counselor, Sue Won talked about her upset with her father and her conflicted feelings toward her mother, whom she loved and respected but feared at the same time. With help, she began to develop a better self-concept, not seeing herself as such an unworthy person. She needed also to work on more practical problems: how to be more disciplined in her schoolwork and how to study more effectively.

Not everyone in a situation like Sue Won's is comfortable talking to a therapist. Living in two distinct cultures and trying to bridge the gap puts you in a difficult position. You feel disloyal, like a traitor, if you talk to someone outside the family. You feel guilty that you have not lived up to your parents' expectations—and yet you need help.

To whom do you turn? You fear that your family will not understand, that they may punish you, if you ask them if you can see a therapist.

You fear to speak to a therapist, not only out of familial loyalty, but you also fear the judgment of the therapist, another adult, another authority figure.

In addition, psychotherapy itself can pose problems for your ethnic identity. Becoming a self-fulfilled, self-directed person may be a goal in Western or American psychotherapy, but it may not be an ideal to strive for within the culture of your family. The family unit may come before the desires of the individual. You may feel the pull to be more independent that comes from the larger society, but this may be in conflict with your family's values.

These are issues that can be discussed and worked on in psychotherapy, if you choose to seek that help. But before you do so, you may find it better to start with some trusted adult, such as a counselor or teacher, someone who understands both cultures and can give you direction.

But whatever you decide . . .

- Don't be like Sue Won and keep everything to yourself.
- Don't rely on wild dramatic actions to win attention and sympathy.
- Do find someone to talk to.
- Do find someone who can help you to find solutions to your problems.
- Do find someone who can make you feel good about yourself.

PARENTS WHO ARE TOO CLOSE

Sometimes parents may want so much to help you that they feel they should take over *all* your problems. This may have been okay when you were quite small. But as you get older, parents' help with all of life's problems becomes less necessary and may even inhibit your personal growth and sense of self-confidence. Learning to separate from one's parents is a natural part of development, which starts even when you are a very small child.

On some level parents know this, but it may be hard for them to admit that you are growing up or that you are growing away from them. Your parents may feel so responsible for you or so bonded to you that it is painful for them to let someone else get close to you.

Parent or Friend?

Sometimes a parent wants to be your best friend as well as your parent. Frequently this is a mother-daughter situation, but not always. In such situations for example, you the child tell your mother all your secrets, and she talks openly to you about her life. This is likely to happen if there is no father living in the family, perhaps after a divorce. The closeness makes you feel special, and you feel you are helping your mother as well.

You may like that feeling of being special to your parent, of being privy to her feelings and having her know everything about you. Your parent has become like your best friend.

But sometimes it can become a burden as your mother tells you intimate details of her life, complains about your father, and uses you as her closest friend. Personal boundaries become blurred in this interdependent relationship. You begin to feel responsible for her, for her happiness. And she becomes more bonded to you and more dependent on you the child.

If you decide to go for counseling or therapy, you may even feel guilty confiding in someone else, sharing family secrets. You may feel even more guilty saying negative things about your parents. Yet sometimes that is one of the issues that you need to work on for your own growth and independence. You may also feel guilty for deserting your mother, particularly if she has few friends or family to turn to.

The parent who has become very involved in your life may not always be the person that you want to share your secrets with. Perhaps you have always told your mother everything, but now that you are getting older you realize there are things that you do not want her to know, things that are too personal, that you want to handle on your own. You feel sure that your mother would be upset if she knew you were keeping a secret from her. Yet you are beginning to feel that you need this distance, this independence from her. Unfortunately, you may have to be the one to make the first move. You may have to educate her about what you need.

As one student put it, "She can be a friend as a mother, but what I really want is a *mother* as a friend." In the same vein, how often I have heard students lament: "I need a mother, not a friend."

TALKING TO YOUR BROTHER OR SISTER

Having a close relationship with a brother or sister can be very reassuring. You have someone in the family, someone close with whom you can share your worries and fears. A sibling can be a special person in time of need:

He or she has the advantage of being a member of the family, so issues of family loyalty or shame are lessened.

Also your sibling knows you for a long time, knows your parents, may live at home with you, and has shared many of your growing-up experiences. But you must be aware that even those who grow up in the same home have not really had the same exact experiences.

Different experiences. For one thing, your siblings have had different experiences with your parents. If a sibling is older than you, the situation may have been different when he was your age. Perhaps the financial situation was better or worse; perhaps your parents were living together, or fighting less. Perhaps your father was or was not an alcoholic at that time. Because of the many differences in the family environment from one time to another, the lives of children who grow up in the same home are still quite different in many aspects.

Different personalities. Parents can react to children differently, partly because children have different personalities. You and your sister, or you and your brother have different personalities. Were they caused by the way you were treated in the family? Or did your different ways of reacting cause your parents to respond to you in different ways?

The answer is probably a little of each. Infants seem to be born with different personalities; some are cranky, some quiet, some alert, some happy. But these little personalities can be molded by the way others react to them. The different moods and ways of responding begin a cycle of interaction within a family that continues throughout life.

Different Roles in the Family.   Eventually the children take on their own particular role within the family. They may eventually be designated the bright one, the pretty one, the lazy one, the good one, or the bad one. You may recognize yourself having one of these labels in your family. Family roles or labels, although not always openly stated, can have long-term effects on how you think of yourself. They can affect your self-concept. You may begin acting that role, in effect validating the self-fulfilling prophecy.

Given all these differences, a brother or sister can be someone to whom you turn in times of distress. Sometimes they can be very helpful, and within the family may act toward you like a parent. That may be something that you need: your brother or sister listening to you, advising you, feeling for you. But in the role of parent they may also criticize you or be too bossy, something that you feel you could live without just now.

CONFIDING IN A FRIEND

Friends can be very helpful with many problems, particularly those involving school or friendships. They are near your age and may understand what is happening and how you may be feeling. But since they are not you, they may be able to provide some distance, some perspective on your problem. When they are your age, they usually can understand much of what you are going through and can sympathize with you. When they are older, you have the wisdom of their life experiences to guide you.

But there are limits to how much a friend can help. For one thing, knowing you, they may not be unbiased about their opinions. They have their own personal issues that may get in the way of their advice and support. They may also feel that you owe them time and energy to listen and help them with their problems as well. You may not always be able to return the favor when they need it. And after a while they may grow tired of your problems, particularly if they are problems that seem to go on and on and never get better or change. You also have no guarantee that a friend will not reveal a secret. Sometimes it is hard not to share information with others, particularly if it is upsetting information. It is asking a lot of friends to keep it all to themselves.

Then again there may be things that you just can't bring yourself to tell a friend, something that you are ashamed of. You might find yourself feeling awkward when you see your friend in school or socially. In such cases, it may be time to seek help from an objective third party, one trained to evaluate and help you with problems.

CHAPTER 5

What's the Difference between Counseling and Psychotherapy?

You may feel better after talking to a parent or a friend who can listen to your problems, be understanding, and give you some advice if need be. Sometimes a teacher, community leader, or a member of the clergy can be helpful. Many religious leaders have had training in *pastoral counseling*, which enables them to help people with some of their personal problems.

Sometimes it makes you feel special when these adults take an interest in you, and their attention can be very rewarding and give you needed confidence. Their advice may also be just want you need. If you have to deal with these people on an everyday basis, however, you may not want to share your innermost secrets and deepest feelings with them. You may not be certain how they will react, and you may feel awkward when you see them again. Thus, you may want to talk to someone who is not directly involved in your immediate life, someone who can offer confidentiality and who has special training to help with psychological, interpersonal, and behavioral issues.

Now that you are thinking of getting some kind of professional help, you may be a bit confused. Counseling? Therapy? What's the difference, you may be asking. If I wanted to go for help I wouldn't even know where to start. Well, join the club. Most people, adults included, don't understand the differences.

That's partly because there is a lot of overlap between counseling and psychotherapy. Both are interventions in which you go to someone when you have problems to discuss and work out. But there are differences.

Counseling usually, although not always, focuses on more short-term practical issues about which you are looking for advice and guidance.

Psychotherapy is usually more intense and takes longer. It is for more serious personal problems.

With both interventions you talk over your problems with a trained professional. That's great, you may be saying to yourself, but . . .

HOW DO I KNOW WHICH INTERVENTION TO CHOOSE?

To know if you should be considering counseling or psychotherapy, it is helpful to distinguish between:

(a) acute problems, and
(b) longstanding problems.

Acute Problems

Acute problems are those that have occurred recently and are different from what you usually are struggling with.
For example:

- You have done poorly on an important test.
- You just broke up with your girlfriend or boyfriend.
- You had a fight with your father.

In most cases, acute problems can be handled by talking to a parent or a friend. If you continue to feel upset about them, a teacher or school counselor can advise you. But if they become very serious and start to interfere with your life, a psychotherapist is probably needed to help you.

Longstanding Problems

Longstanding problems are those that keep coming back or just never seem to go away. These problems are best treated by a mental health professional, that is, a psychotherapist. Such problems may also involve school or relationships, like those described above, but they seem to be always a part of your life and never get any better:

- You always feel an underlying sadness or are very nervous.
- You have an eating disorder.
- You are using drugs.
- You are drinking too much.

- You have fears that others think are irrational.
- You have a general sense of uneasiness without knowing why.

These are only a handful of the possible problems that a person might have that could be helped by a trained therapist. Others are suggested in the personal self-quizzes in Chapter 2.

COUNSELING

When you go to a trained professional for counseling you are usually looking for guidance about a specific problem or choices that you need to make about school, jobs, or your future. Counseling is usually short-term (one to five sessions), and the counselor takes an active role in the process, giving advice and information. In counseling the problem is usually specific and well defined, such as:

- what courses to take?
- what colleges to apply to?
- what to do after graduation?
- how to study better?

The counselor at your school has had special training to help you make these decisions and knows about books and other resources where you can find answers. Sometimes school counselors give you interest inventories or other tests to help you understand yourself better, so you can make good choices. Or you may choose to go to a vocational counselor outside of school to help you make decisions about your future.

School counselors also have training in child development and are aware of the many personal and social problems that students face. They are there to help you if you are having problems with teachers, friends, or parents. They are prepared to help you with the more "acute" problems.

The school counselor may suggest that you see the school psychologist to take some psychological tests. These tests will give more information about your abilities or personal strengths and weaknesses, so that you can be referred for the appropriate kind of help. The issue of testing is discussed in Chapter 14.

If your problems are more serious and longstanding, the school counselor will probably suggest that you see a mental health professional for psychotherapy outside of school.

PSYCHOTHERAPY

When your problems make you feel very bad or have been with you for a long time, you need to consider the kind of help that will get to the root of the problem. Advice and guidance don't seem to be enough. After a while you are back to feeling the same way, doing the same things, and the problems just don't go away. By getting to the root of the problem, you gain insight into your motivations, and you are able to make changes in your life, in your behavior, and in your personality.

The different kinds of psychotherapy are discussed in the next chapter, but essentially they differ from counseling in that in psychotherapy you are not going just for advice and guidance. You are not looking for answers, but for understanding.

- You seek major changes in your life and your personality.

- You seek solutions to problems and feelings that have been with you for a long time.

Because these changes are basic to who you are, the process of psychotherapy may be longer and slower than counseling. The therapist is more like a guide who will help you in this process of self-discovery.

CHAPTER 6

The Different Kinds
of Psychotherapy

Psychotherapists select from among many forms of psychotherapy depending upon their training and the patient's needs. To better understand the process of therapy, let us look at some of the terminology and the methods used. There is a lot of overlap in some of the approaches, and often it does not matter much which approach the therapist uses, as long as the therapist is well trained and experienced.

PSYCHOTHERAPY

Psychotherapy is a psychological intervention or therapeutic technique that is based on the idea of talking through your problems with a mental health professional. Originally this technique was a "talking therapy," in which you the client were helped by talking about your life with a therapist. Over the years variants of psychotherapy have evolved.

PSYCHOANALYSIS

Psychoanalysis is the original form of psychotherapy, which was developed in the early part of the twentieth century by the Austrian doctor Sigmund Freud. Many people incorrectly use the term *psychoanalysis* to refer to psychotherapy. Actually, psychoanalysis has its own special methods that distinguish it from the other psychotherapies.

Adults, rather than teenagers and children, usually go into psychoanalysis, since the main focus is more on helping you to understand your past and how your basic character has been formed. With young people, this technique may be used when a person's development has been thwarted in some way and the young person needs to develop a basic sense of self and to have better relationships with others.

The basic method of psychoanalysis is "free association," in which you are encouraged to express everything that comes into your mind, no matter what. The therapist says very little except to ask questions or to restate for you what you seem to be saying.

The fact that the therapist (or psychoanalyst) is not more active can be quite frustrating for some patients. Yet in this method the frustration and how you feel about the therapist are central to the treatment. Essentially, you focus on your past; your current problems are only starting points to a more systematic exploration of the roots of your important relationships with others.

In psychoanalysis, the analysand (patient) usually lies down on a couch during the session and looks off into space or closes his/her eyes while talking. The analyst sits on a chair behind your head, so as to be out of your line of view. In this way you are not distracted and are free to talk about what you will.

Psychoanalysis is very intense and usually requires four or five sessions a week for 50 minutes each. This type of therapy is long-term and may take from three to eight years to complete the analysis of yourself. Thus, it is a major commitment in time and money. Although it may be costly, it can be affordable: Psychoanalytic training institutes in some of the larger cities often provide low-cost therapy, with trainee therapists acting as analysts.

The other types of psychotherapy have had early origins in psychoanalysis but are much different in focus and method. For one, the therapists in the other methods interact with you more readily, although you are expected usually to do most of the talking and most of the work.

PSYCHODYNAMIC PSYCHOTHERAPY

Psychodynamic psychotherapy is probably the most common form of psychotherapy practiced in the United States. The focus of this approach is to help you understand why you behave and feel as you do by exploring your past experiences and relationships.

Psychodynamic psychotherapy differs from psychoanalysis in several ways. The therapy is usually not so intense, usually requiring only one or two sessions a week. The therapist is more active, and you do not lie on a couch but sit facing your therapist. The frustrations and feelings toward your therapist do not play as large a role in your learning to understand yourself as they do in psychoanalysis. Psychodynamic therapy focuses on conflicts in your personal and interpersonal life. Although it draws upon your past, that is not the main focus but just one of the areas covered to help you deal with your present situation.

In psychodynamic psychotherapy you talk about relationships you have had with significant people in your life, and you try to understand how these relationships are influencing the way you are acting with other people now.

- If you have trouble trusting other people, perhaps someone in your past let you down, hurt you in some way. Now you have trouble trusting anyone.
- Perhaps because of an earlier feeling of being rejected or abandoned by someone, you now do everything in your power to make people like you. You dislike yourself for this. You almost feel like a "doormat," but you don't seem able to help yourself.

By talking things over with the therapist, you gain insight and understanding of the conflicts that may be contributing to the way you feel. Problems with your current relationships with family, friends, and others are a main focus of this type of therapy.

The therapist lets you do most of the talking and tries not to direct you too much so as not to influence what you want to say. The therapist is essentially a trained listener who will ask you leading questions or make comments about what you have said. This forces you to rethink what you have just said or done, and you gain different ideas. In addition, you learn to see your life in a different way and to find solutions to your problems. You, however, do the work in therapy; the therapist is your guide.

At first you may not like this approach. You want someone to give you advice, answers. But there are probably a lot of people in your life giving you advice, telling you what to do. The reason therapy is different is that here you learn to explore for yourself and to take control of your own life. If others tell you all the time what to do, you will never learn the techniques of self-examination and self-control.

The therapist does guide you, however, and will make observations and interpretations of things that you say. The therapist may point out times when you seem angry with someone or upset with yourself. You may discover that you tend to react in certain ways because of something that happened to you in the past. This may surprise you.

Then you may think, but so what if I learn why I act this way? By understanding that your feelings and behaviors are not just accidents, that they have a reason, you gain much control over your life. This knowledge may let you realize that you are not a bad person, that there are reasons why you act as you do.

Also, this knowledge enables you to try to change the way you act or think. It gives you control. You do not have to be afraid that things will get out of control, that they are happening for no reason at all.

A Course in Yourself

Essentially, psychodynamic psychotherapy is like a course in school—except that in this case *you* are the subject. Through the process of therapy:

- you learn who you are;
- you analyze what happened to you in the past; and
- you come to see how it affects you today.

Through therapy:

- you gain an understanding of your behavior and your emotions, and

- you learn how to change if you want to.

Making Changes

You may be thinking: "I don't want therapy to change me. That will make me like everyone else." That is a common misconception. The purpose of psychotherapy is not to try to make you "fit in," or to be like everyone else. Through psychotherapy you learn about aspects of yourself that make you . . . **you**. You may like some of these traits and not like others. You may learn to appreciate yourself more. You may discover things about yourself that you don't want to change, parts of yourself that you now take pride in. Perhaps you will even become more creative, more interested in life and in other people. Eventually you will learn how to keep those parts of yourself that you like and to modify or get rid of the ones you don't like. The decision is essentially yours.

BEHAVIORAL THERAPY

The focus of behavioral therapy is to change unwanted behaviors. Behavior therapy is useful for many specific situations and in treating unwanted behaviors, such as phobias and anxiety. The techniques include:

Relaxation Exercises

These exercises can take various forms:

Systematic desensitization, in which you learn to concentrate on parts of your body, relaxing individual muscles starting with your feet and working up through your body to your head.

Imagery, in which you are told to think of situations or places that are soothing to you. The therapist (or a tape of the therapist's voice) makes suggestions about what you might think about, for example, a beautiful beach. You are told to imagine the scene, think about every detail, feel your body lying on the warm sand, feel the cool breeze on your face, the water touching your toes.

Both of these techniques require that you focus your attention on what you are doing at the moment. You have no room in your mind for worries; you concentrate on relaxing your muscles. Such exercises are quite helpful for people who are under stress or are having problems sleeping.

Behavior Modification

This term refers to techniques that might include imagining or role-playing a new way of behaving in the safety of the therapist's office. When you feel comfortable with this new way of acting, the therapist suggests certain behaviors for you to try out outside of therapy and to report the result at the next session. Gradually you come to see that others respond well to your new behaviors and that you are able to achieve what you want. In essence you receive rewards and not the expected punishments from others, and thus learn new ways of behaving.

Flooding

In this technique you put yourself in a situation that you fear. Sometimes the therapist comes with you. The idea is that the anxiety or fear will gradually disappear if you learn that nothing terrible will happen to you. Flooding has been helpful, for example, for people who are afraid of closed-in spaces or crowds. They begin by imagining the situation, for example, standing in a crowded elevator. The next step is actually to go into an elevator, at first with your therapist, then on your own. Gradually you learn that you can handle these situations and not panic.

Modeling

In this technique you observe someone else doing what you are afraid of doing. Often the therapist acts as the model. This technique has been used effectively, for example, with people who are afraid of animals. Seeing other children or the therapist approach an animal that they are afraid of helps them to feel more in control and to overcome their fears. Role-playing in therapy and watching how others behave in social situations outside therapy are techniques that play a part in modeling.

Assertiveness and Social Skills Training

Here you analyze your own patterns of behavior and try out new skills. You learn specific ways of responding appropriately, of expressing your opinions and your needs. For example, you may have trouble speaking in class, asking someone for a date, going for a job interview, telling someone you don't like what they're doing, or speaking up for yourself in certain situations.

Assertiveness training makes use of role-playing in which you act out various roles in therapy with the help of the therapist. You are also given suggestions about things to do or say outside of therapy. At the next session, you discuss how you felt being more assertive and what happened. Gradually you learn step by step to change your behavior and to become more self-confident.

COGNITIVE THERAPY

The basic focus of cognitive therapy is to help you to see the role that your thoughts play in your behavior and your feelings about yourself. Emotional problems are thought to come from distorted and self-defeating ways of thinking. Through therapy you learn to identify these negative thoughts and replace them with more realistic ones. The theory is that by changing your thought patterns, your feelings and behavior will change as well. Cognitive therapy is a helpful approach for treating certain kinds of depression.

The cognitive therapist is very active in the sessions and acts much like a teacher or tutor. You are even given exercises and homework to do each week.

Cognitive Restructuring

Through this technique you learn to modify your emotional responses by changing (or *reframing*) your thoughts. For example, you may think that a friend has been avoiding you. You think to yourself: "She must not like me." Then you make the "cognitive" jump to: "No one likes me." And then you generalize further to: "I am unlovable."

Thus, you go through life feeling just that way— unloved. It is as though you are looking for examples to fulfill your negative ideas of yourself. You interpret others' behavior in a bad or negative way.

After talking this over with your therapist, you may discover that these are *automatic thoughts* that seem to pop into your mind every time something doesn't go right for you. Your therapist will help you to see this pattern or *schema*, as they call it.

You may then be asked to test the validity of these

negative thoughts, in this case by asking your friend directly why she didn't come over to sit with you the other day. You may learn that her reason is not what you expected.

Through cognitive therapy you learn not to attribute motivations to others. You know only what *you* feel. Even though you know other people well, you can't assume that you always understand what goes on in their minds or why they act the way they do.

You may be asked to keep an ongoing list of your negative thoughts and the situations in which they occur. Then you replace each negative thought with a more positive one. This is called *reframing*.

In our example, you might say:

"Perhaps my friend is having problems of her own and it has nothing to do with me."

"Maybe she wasn't feeling well, or felt awkward because I was with someone else."

"It doesn't mean that I am unlovable just because someone doesn't want to be with me."

Remind yourself: "I am a good person."
                           "I am lovable."

Make a list of your good traits:
I am . . .
        __courteous
        __funny
        __bright
        __good-looking
        __interesting
        __a good listener

    ___athletic

    ___or whatever your good traits are.

If you find it hard to list them, your therapist can help you. Everyone has good traits; if you can't list any, it is a sign that you probably do need to speak to someone who can help you understand yourself and improve your self-perception.

Cognitive Rehearsal

This technique is similar to that used in behavior therapy in which you think of a situation that bothers you, then you imagine in detail different ways of dealing with it; e.g., what else you might say or do. In a sense you rehearse the situation mentally to change the way you think about it. Then you go on to change the way you act and feel.

Although cognitive therapy is similar in many ways to behavior therapy, it differs in that in cognitive therapy you change the way you think about something, and that is supposed to change the way your behave and—as a by-product—how you feel. In behavior therapy, you focus on changing the behavior itself, which in turn is supposed to change the way you think and feel. Cognitive therapy starts with the thoughts; the other, with the behavior. The outcomes can be the same.

The techniques of cognitive and behavior therapy are often used by psychodynamic therapists, and cognitive and behavior therapists may borrow techniques from some of the other therapies as well. That is why it is sometimes good to find a therapist who is "eclectic," who is familiar with the various approaches and uses techniques from each as appropriate.

OTHER APPROACHES

Other approaches or therapies include Jungian, gestalt, and rational emotive therapy. Before seeing the therapist, you can ask what kind of philosophy he or she espouses and what techniques are used in practice. If you need more information about that type of therapy, you can consult some of the books listed in the back of this book or others that are available in libraries or bookstores.

Therapists often have specialties as well, and some specialize in working with children and adolescents. When making the appointment or at the first interview, you can inquire how much experience or training the therapist has with people of your age. Many therapists, particularly psychologists, have training and experience in child psychology, even though they have not actually specialized in that area.

FORMATS

In addition to the various approaches to psychotherapy, there are also different formats in which you can be seen: individual, group, and family therapy.

Individual Therapy

In psychodynamic, behavioral, and cognitive therapy, you generally meet alone with the therapist, usually once or twice a week for 45- or 50-minute sessions. In psychoanalysis, which is very intense, you are usually asked to come four or five times a week for 50 minutes each session. How long you will need to continue in psychotherapy depends upon the nature of your problem.

Brief or Short-Term Psychotherapy

Some problems can be dealt with in a few sessions. This is usually so if you are working on an acute issue or a specific problem. If it is school-related, for example, it may take only a few sessions for you to deal with the situation. Often, however, brief psychotherapy takes from 12 to 20 sessions, as you must first gain an understanding of the problem and then learn to ways of dealing with it.

Long-Term Psychotherapy

Most often psychodynamic psychotherapy is open-ended: There is no set number of sessions, and you continue to talk about your problems until you feel that you have gained enough insight and control to move on. Long-term therapy can last a year or more. This may be because the problems are longstanding and you need time to uncover the reasons and to work out the solutions and changes. The problems may be so serious or severe that there is a lot of resistance to opening up, so the process may be slow as you gradually become able to talk about them. The therapy may go on for years, because as you learn to deal with problems, you uncover others that you would like to work on. At certain points in the therapy, you and the therapist reevaluate how you are doing and decide whether there are other issues that you would like to talk about, or if it is time to terminate therapy.

Group Therapy

In group therapy you get together with five to eight people to talk about your common problems. A trained professional helps guide the session. Group therapy can be helpful in making you feel that you are not alone and in learning how others handle their problems. If you are having difficulties dealing with other people you can also learn relationship skills through the group process.

Support Groups

Related to group therapy are support groups in which people share ideas but do not necessarily probe into each other's personal lives, motivations, and feelings. A trained leader may or may not be involved in a support group. Support groups are often used in treating drug and alcohol abuse and physical and sexual abuse. Children also may participate in support groups if they become ill, or if a parent becomes ill or dies.

Family Therapy

In family therapy, as the name implies, members of the family get together to improve communication and to work out a problem that has developed within the family system. A family therapist, who is often a psychologist or social worker, facilitates the interchange.

In most cases, family therapy is for a limited amount of time, e.g., six weeks to six months. Sessions can be once a week, once every other week, or as time goes on as infrequent as once a month.

Your parents may suggest that you come with them for family therapy if there has been some kind of crisis in the family, an ongoing family problem, poor relationships between family members, and a breakdown in communication. These problems can cover a host of issues such as:

- alcoholism in the family (you or a parent)
- divorce or separation

- problems with stepparents or stepsiblings
- moving to a new home
- illness in the family.

Family therapy may be suggested when members are not getting along. Young people often act out when there is some kind of stress in the family and become the "identified patient." You may feel that it is not you but they who need help, and in some cases you may be right. But it may be your behavior that is drawing the attention. You may be talking back to your parents, or not observing curfew. Or you may be using drugs, drinking too much, or getting into arguments with other family members.

Whatever the reason, if family therapy is suggested, you may see it as a form of punishment. In most cases, however, when parents finally decide to go into therapy with their children they are looking for help and a solution to the problem. Both you and they can benefit.

Verlene

Verlene resented her mother's new boyfriend, Ron. She usually stayed in her room when she knew he was coming over. She hated seeing his toothbrush and razor in the bathroom, and one day in a rage she threw them into the wastebasket. It took a while for her mother to figure out what Verlene had done, and she was made to apologize to Ron. That only infuriated Verlene further. She felt that her mother loved him more than she loved her daughter, and this only proved it.

The next day when the postman arrived and she saw that Ron was now getting mail at her house, she was beside herself. Taking a match, she set his mail on fire and watched happily as it burned. Later she heard her mother and Ron discussing his missing mail. No one suspected.

Then one day when she was having an argument with her mother, she blurted out how much she hated both of them and revealed that she had burned his mail. It gave her a feeling of power and revenge even though she realized that the revelation was going bring her a lot of grief. As she expected, her mother was furious with her and demanded that she apologize. This time Verlene took to her room, refusing to talk to anyone.

The next day after her mother had calmed down, she told Verlene that she had spoken to a family therapist and wanted Verlene to come with her and Ron for family therapy. Verlene was angry. She felt that she was being punished again. She didn't like Ron, didn't like him in the house, didn't want him in her life. She felt she had no control over what went on, that her wishes didn't count, and that she was losing her mother.

Feeling she had no choice, she reluctantly went to family therapy with her mother. There Verlene sat, sullen, her arms folded, looking at the floor. She gave only one-word answers when the therapist addressed a question to her. After a while the therapist asked to speak to each of them separately for a few minutes.

When it was Verlene's time, she was again silent. But the therapist seemed genuinely concerned; he did not seem to be taking her mother's side as she had thought at first. Gradually Verlene began telling him what had happened, and why she had acted this way. She told him how she felt about Ron and her mother. She found herself beginning to cry, the first time she had allowed herself to cry in a long time.

The therapist asked her what she didn't like about Ron, how she'd like things to change. Then he reconvened the family.

In the individual talks, the therapist had been able to draw each person out, to elicit their feelings. Verlene became aware that they were all misunderstanding each other. Out of frustration and anger, Verlene had been acting in upsetting ways. Her mother and Ron had begun to see Verlene as selfish and stubborn. Her mother even worried about Verlene's sanity.

Given her behavior, Verlene could see how they could reach that conclusion. And when she finally did talk about her own feelings, her mother seemed to listen and hold back the anger that had surfaced at home. The therapist had a way of asking questions and explaining things that made them much clearer. Somehow everything seemed to be more in control.

Verlene still didn't like Ron, or at least didn't like him being in the house so much. Her mother agreed for the time to limit Ron's visits and to let Verlene know when he would be coming. Verlene and her mother agreed to spend at least one afternoon together over the weekend doing things that they enjoyed doing together.

Homework. As is often the case in family therapy, the therapist gave them homework, exercises that the family members were to do in the week before the next session. In this case, Verlene and her mother were each to do one nice thing for the other during the week. It was to be a surprise, something special. For the time being, Ron was left out, as the first exercise was to rebuild the relationship between Verlene and her mother.

It is hard to think of special surprises, particularly when you are angry with the other person. Having to plan for the surprise caused Verlene to spend some time thinking of her mother's needs. She found herself wondering what her mother would do for her. It had been a long time since she had felt a part of her mother's attention in that way. And it wasn't like a punishment at all. The special surprises gave them both something to look forward to and helped them to appreciate each other.

As time went on, the relationship between mother and daughter began to improve, as each took more time to try to understand the other. It was several months before they decided they didn't need therapy any more. There were still the tensions, but now communication had been opened up.

This case study gives you an idea of the kind of problem that may be brought to family therapy. It also shows that you can use family therapy to your own advantage, that it is a place for you to deal with your problems and try to improve communication with others in your family. It may feel like punishment, and you may feel you have been singled out as the bad one. You may be afraid that everyone will focus on you and that the therapist will side with your parents or someone else. That is not the way it should be in family therapy: The problem is seen as a problem within the family system, with each person playing a role.

If you are acting out and are identified as the "patient" at first, it may be that that is the only way you have of calling attention to a bigger problem in the family. A family therapist will try to find out what is going on. You may not even know yourself what is the problem. You may be upset by your parents' frequent fighting, or what you see as favoritism toward a brother or sister, without realizing that that is what is bothering you.

It is usually good for young people who are in family therapy to be in individual therapy at the same time. In this way you have someone to talk to who really does know you—your therapist. And you have a place where you can talk freely about feelings and problems that you are not comfortable talking about in front of others, even your parents.

CHAPTER 7

How Do Psychotherapists Differ?

Psychotherapists or mental health professionals are trained to assist you with different kinds of problems:

- emotional (how you are feeling)
- interpersonal (how you are getting along with others)
- behavioral (how you are acting).

However, the treatment you receive may differ depending upon the psychotherapist's training.

To help you understand and to make an informed choice, I shall give a brief description of some of the differences in training and practice. Who knows: After reading about these therapists and how they train, maybe you'll want to be one someday?

ONE WORD OF CAUTION

Remember: any one who practices "psychotherapy" can call himself or herself a *psychotherapist*. The title itself tells you nothing about a person's training and experience, nor does it mean that the person has any particular credentials. The title is often used by persons who have little or no training. For that reason, it is essential to inquire specifically about the therapist's background to assure yourself that you are getting someone qualified to help you.

Now let us look at some of the qualifications and training for professionals practicing psychotherapy.

QUALIFICATIONS AND TRAINING

You may be familiar with some of the kinds of therapists: psychologist, psychiatrist, social worker, school counselor—What's the difference?

Psychologists

Psychologists provide various types of psychotherapy (individual, group, and family). They are also qualified to administer psychological tests, which are discussed more fully in Chapter 14.

These professionals receive their education at a university graduate school and usually have a doctorate (PhD, EdD, or PsyD) in Psychology, specializing in an area such as Clinical Psychology or Counseling Psychology.

Their graduate studies take about three or four years

after college and include courses such as abnormal psychology, developmental and child psychology, personality theory, and psychological testing.

While in graduate school students begin treating patients or clients under the supervision of their professors. Later they do a full year's internship, during which they work at a hospital or other mental health facility treating people who have psychological problems. Those who pursue the PhD must write a dissertation, which is a lengthy paper based on a clinical or research project.

After receiving their degree, they must also pass a state examination in psychology, at which time they become certified or licensed to practice as a psychologist in that state. In most states only those who have been licensed or certified by the state in which they practice are entitled to call themselves psychologists.

In some cases a psychologist may have a master's degree (MA, MS or MEd), which requires only one or two years of graduate study. Therapists with only a master's degree in psychology may be required to work under the supervision of a state certified psychologist, if they are not eligible to become licensed or certified in their state.

School Psychologists

School psychologists are psychologists who have had special graduate training in education and child development. As part of their training they must do an internship, where they work for a semester under supervision in a public school. School psychologists may have either a master's degree, which they receive usually after two or three years of study, or a doctorate (PhD or EdD), which is described in the previous section.

School psychologists are hired by school districts and

work in the school setting with children who have learning disabilities, academic problems, or emotional difficulties. They administer psychological tests, such as intelligence tests and aptitude tests to help place students in special programs. They may also administer personality or vocational aptitude tests to guide students who need help with problems or in making choices about their future.

Psychiatrists

Psychiatrists are medical doctors (MD) who have taken a specialty in psychiatry. After college, these students have pursued four years of medical school, followed by a year's internship at a hospital, which may include some exposure to patients who have been hospitalized for severe emotional problems (for example, clinical depression, schizophrenia, psychosis, paranoia, impulse disorders). To become psychiatrists, they must do an additional three years of clinical training, called a residency in psychiatry. This usually consists of treating mentally ill patients in a hospital setting under the supervision of senior psychiatrists. Here they receive training in psychotherapy and learn about pharmacology, the treating of certain mental illnesses or disorders with medication.

In addition to obtaining their medical license they must pass state board examinations after the residency in order to call themselves psychiatrists. This is a protected term, which cannot be used by anyone who has not fulfilled the requirements. Many psychiatrists even do further training such as specializing in child psychiatry.

In addition to receiving psychotherapy, you would want to see a psychiatrist if you needed medication for your condition or needed to be hospitalized as part of your care. If you are seeing a nonmedical therapist, such as a psychologist or social worker for your psychotherapy, your therapist can make arrangements for you to consult with a psychiatrist if you need to be on medication. In such cases you would continue to see your therapist for psychotherapy, and the psychiatrist would supervise your medication. See Chapter 13.

Social Workers

Studies for a master's degree in social work (MSW) usually consist of two years of training after college in a School of Social Work. Social workers receive practical training in areas such as welfare, child advocacy, health insurance benefits, and placement after hospitalization. Some, but not all, school programs include supervised training in psychotherapy.

In most states social workers can become certified (CSW) or licensed (LICSW) following two additional years of supervised training and the passing of a state examination. Some social workers also go on for a doctor's degree (DSW).

Psychiatric Nurses

After nurse's training a nurse must pass a state examination to be licensed or registered in the profession (RN). The term psychiatric nurse refers to a nurse who works in a psychiatric ward in a hospital or in an outpatient mental health clinic. There is at this time no special license in psychiatric nursing.

Some schools of nursing now offer specialized training in psychiatric nursing, and some state nursing associations award a certificate in that area to those who have taken certain courses and have had certain relevant experience.

Although some psychiatric nurses do have private practices in psychotherapy, the title psychiatric nurse does not necessarily mean that the person has fulfilled any specific training or has any particular qualifications in that area.

Psychoanalysts

Although this term is often used by the general public to mean psychotherapist, it actually refers to therapists who practice a particular type of intensive psychotherapy, developed by Sigmund Freud, called psychoanalysis.

These professionals are usually psychiatrists, psychologists, or social workers who have done additional training at a psychoanalytic institute, where they learn the special techniques for helping people to examine their innermost character.

Others without the extensive graduate training of these mental health professionals can also study at psychoanalytic institutes and are called *lay therapists*. They can be good therapists as well, but they do not always have the depth and breadth of training that the more highly trained therapists do.

Pastoral Counselors

Members of the clergy (ministers, priests, rabbis) offer counseling to their parishioners. Some of these clergy have studied psychological counseling in divinity school or seminary; others have pursued additional training at a training institute or university. The term pastoral counselor, however, is not protected and can be used by anyone, even those without any training at all.

School Counselors

The school counselor is someone who has pursued graduate training after college, specializing in the problems of school-age children. (In some schools they are still referred to as guidance counselors; however, that name is changing as their duties have taken on a larger role than the term "guidance" implies.)

A school counselor usually has a master's degree (MA or MEd) in School Counseling, which can take two to three years of graduate study after college, including an internship working in a school system. Some school counselors go further and get doctor's degrees in their fields. The degree may be a Doctor of Education (EdD), if the studying took place in a university School of Education's Department of School Counseling, rather than a Department of Psychology.

The counselors' work is similar to that of school psychologists, although the counselors are usually less involved in the school's testing programs. School counselors usually do not deal with students' long-term problems or serious mental illnesses, but they are often the mental health person that the student knows best. Thus, they or a teacher can be the first professional outside of the home to know when a student is in distress. If your school counselor can't help you, he or she should be able to get you the kind of help that you need.

Probation Officers

Although not usually included under discussions of mental health professionals, probation officers do a lot of counseling. They usually have a college degree (BS) and have been given on-the-job training. In some cases they may also have a graduate degree such as a master's degree in counseling or another field,

Substance Abuse Counselors

Mental health professionals can get specialized training in substance abuse counseling, either for drug or alcohol abuse. Some states have special programs and requirements to become an alcoholism counselor. Courses must be taken and many hours of work with alcoholics must be undertaken to earn the state certification. The same may be true for drug abuse counseling, depending upon the state.

Substance abuse counselors often work in hospitals, clinics, and mental health and rehabilitation agencies. Many of those who provide counseling to substance abusers have been abusers themselves. They have gone through a recovery program and have specific training in substance abuse counseling, either for drugs or alcohol.

SUMMARY: WHICH PROBLEMS TO TAKE WHERE?

Now when you go to see a counselor or therapist you can have some idea of the differences in qualifications. The differences are for the most part:

1) the amount of training, and
2) the kind of training.

For example, psychiatrists and psychiatric nurses have had medical training. The other therapists and counselors may have studied in counseling or psychology departments in universities; however, as part of their practical experience they also have worked under supervision in hospitals or schools.

Although there is much overlap in the kinds of problems these professionals can treat, the following summary will give you a general idea of the services they can offer.

Summary of Services

Psychologists
— Psychotherapy for
  • long-standing or serious emotional problems, or
  • short-term therapy for acute problems.
— Psychological and vocational testing.

Psychiatrists
— Psychotherapy for longstanding psychological problems and serious mental illness.
— Medication for depression or other psychiatric conditions.
— Admission to hospitals for psychiatric care.

Counselors
— Counseling for problems of everyday life
  • problems with your school work,
  • problems with teachers or other students,
  • concerns about your future, such as, where to go to college, or what kind of job to prepare for.

Social workers and psychiatric nurses
— Counseling for
  • acute problems in your everyday life,
— Providing information about
  • community resources or
  • special programs for yourself or others in your family.
  • psychotherapy, depending upon the individual's training.

Substance abuse counselors
— Counseling for:
  • dependency upon drugs or
  • problems controlling your use of alcohol.

Probation officers
— Assigned if you have had trouble with the law.
— Monitor your behavior
— Counsel you regarding life situations.

Within their fields therapists use different approaches or methods. It is important to note that research suggests that the actual approach used may not be as important as the therapist's training and experience. Also, most therapists borrow from the different approaches and techniques, even though they may use one particular method more than the others.

CHAPTER ◇ 8

How Do I Find a

Therapist?

IN AN EMERGENCY

You may need to find a therapist in a hurry. Perhaps
there is a crisis in your family or at school. Perhaps
you or someone you know is very depressed or
feeling suicidal. People often speak of suicide when they
are depressed, and that does not necessarily mean that
they will actually try to kill themselves. But since you are
not a professional you have no way of evaluating such
statements.

If you feel that this is an emergency, the first thing to
do if you can is:

• *Tell your parents or another adult that you trust.*

If someone is being violent, or you are afraid the person
may hurt or kill himself or someone else, immediately go
to a phone:

- *Call the operator by dialing "O",* or
- *Dial "911" in some communities for emergency.*
  Tell the person who answers
  a. who you are,
  b. where you are calling from, and
  c. what the problem is.

If the problem is not an immediate emergency, you may:

- *look in the Yellow Pages* or
- *call information (555-1212 or 411)* to get an appropriate number, such as a
  Hot line for
    suicide
    rape or incest
    substance abuse
    alcoholism
    child abuse
    physical abuse

It's usually better to look for help when you think it is an emergency or a crisis, rather than waiting because you're not sure. It is better to have alerted someone to the possibilities of a problem, even if it turns out that it wasn't an emergency or a problem after all.

WHERE TO FIND HELP

Now let us look at the situations when there is time to do some research. The question about finding a therapist really has two parts:

- Where to find a therapist.

- How to know if he or she is the right person for you?

This second question is dealt with in Chapter 9.

LOCATING A THERAPIST

Ask Others

A word-of-mouth referral is often the best way to find a good professional.

Get a referral from someone who knows the therapist, either from having been a patient or having worked with him or her on a professional level. You may ask:

- your parents
- another trusted adult or family friend
- the school counselor
- the school psychologist
- a trusted teacher
- a minister, rabbi, priest
- your doctor
- a friend who has been seeing a therapist.

Telephone Book or Operator

Look in the Yellow Pages of the telephone book or call the information operator for directory assistance.

Referral sources may be listed under different headings, depending upon where you live and the resources that are available. If you live in a large city, the variety may be so large that it can be confusing at first. In a smaller community or rural area, your choices may be more limited.

Try some of the following headings to see if they are

listed. Any of them may be able to suggest a therapist, support group, or mental health clinic.

- Crisis Services
- Hot Lines
- Information and Referral Services
- Suicide Prevention
- Rape Crisis
- Drug Crisis
- Alcohol Information Referral Service
- Child Abuse
- Runaways
- Community Mental Health Centers
  (*Community mental health centers* may be affiliated with a hospital or be on their own as part of a state system. They may also be private mental health centers.)
- Social Services

In the Appendix you will find the addresses and phone numbers of national agencies that may be able to refer you to someone in your local area.

Professional Associations

Professional associations are other possible sources of referral. Their offices are usually located in your state capital. For example, in New York State you could try the New York State Psychological Association, or the New York State Psychiatric Association in Albany, New York. Just substitute the name of your state and call the information operator for the phone number in your state's capital city.

The national offices of the professional associations

are usually in Washington, DC. They can assist you in finding a therapist in your locality by referring you to a specific therapist, a mental health agency, or the state office of the association. Following are two of the national associations that have resources that may be of help to you:

American Psychological Association
750 First Avenue NE
Washington, DC 20002–4242
(202) 336–5500

American Psychiatric Association
1400 K Street NW
Washington, DC 20005
(202) 682–6000

EXPLAINING THE PROBLEM

Be aware that sometimes the person you first talk to may try to reassure you by telling you that your problems are normal and that you do not need to see a therapist. That indeed may be true, and you may feel better just talking to this person one for a brief time. On the other hand, the person may not really understand what you are feeling or what you are going through. Or that person may feel uncomfortable about therapy in general for personal reasons. If you really do want to talk to someone professionally about your problems, be persistent, and hang in there. Ask someone else from the lists above for a referral.

If you are concerned about a friend but are not sure whether your friend needs help, look over the following list of symptoms or behaviors suggestive of emotional or mental problems to see if they describe your friend. Remember, we all have bad days, but if these signs continue for a while and seem severe, they signal trouble.

THE WARNING SIGNS OF MENTAL ILLNESS

1. Marked personality change
2. Inability to cope with problems and daily activities
3. Strange and grandiose ideas
4. Excessive anxieties
5. Prolonged depressions and apathy
6. Marked changes in eating or sleeping patterns
7. Thinking or talking about suicide
8. Extreme highs and lows
9. Abuse of alcohol or drugs
10. Excessive anger, hostility, or violent behavior
       (from The American Psychiatric Association)

CHAPTER 9

How Do I Evaluate

the Therapist?

To answer this question you need to be able to evaluate the therapist, as well as the psychotherapy itself.

I. *Use reliable sources to find the therapist.*

Follow the steps outlined in Chapter 8:

- Ask people who may know the therapist, or
- Get a referral from recognized agencies.

Even so, you will still not necessarily know if the person is qualified to treat you, or if you will personally like that therapist. So . . .

II. *Ask questions: Interview the therapist.*

You can do this in a polite way, explaining that you want to be sure that he or she is the right person for you. Some of the questions you might ask are:

- "What kind of a therapist are you: a psychologist, psychiatrist, social worker, or what?"
- "Are you licensed or certified in your field in this state?"
  (When you go to see the therapist, a copy of the license should be displayed where you can see it.)
- "Can you tell me about your training? Do you have any special training or experience working with young people?"
- "What type of psychotherapy do you practice? Psychodynamic? Psychoanalytic? Cognitive? Behavioral? Family therapy?"

If the therapist thinks that you won't understand the answers to your own questions, you can explain that you have read a book about psychotherapy, that you have some understanding. Say that you would appreciate his or her answering your questions so you can feel that you are making a good choice.

III. *Ask yourself: Do I feel comfortable with this person?*

It's true that at first it is hard to know if you will like the therapist. That is why it may take a few sessions to be sure. But it is important that you feel comfortable working with the therapist; you need to be able to trust him or her so you can discuss whatever is bothering you.

EVALUATING THE THERAPY PROCESS

The Stages of Therapy

As therapy is a process, you periodically need to evaluate how it is going. Usually, after the first session or so you feel relieved and much better about yourself and your life. But as time goes on you may not always have these highs. You won't necessarily feel happy or good about yourself after each session, as you may be discussing things that are very upsetting to you. That is natural. Also, since therapy is a process, it can take many months for you to notice any change. All that is to be expected.

Making Decisions and Choices

You may be frustrated if the therapist doesn't give you advice, but advice may not be what you need. In many cases, the purpose of therapy is to help you learn to identify your own problems and make your own decisions. If the therapist gives you too much advice, he or she may only be acting like your parents or friends. Then you won't learn to be independent and to do things on your own. And you won't learn that you have choices of your own.

CHANGING THERAPISTS

But if the therapist really doesn't seem to be helping you, it may be time for you to think about changing therapists.

You may feel awkward bringing this up for discussion in therapy, and instead you may just decide to quit without a word. Many people do it this way, but it is not always the best way to proceed.

Talking to the therapist about your feelings and your desire to stop therapy or change therapists:

1. Talking about difficult subjects helps you learn to be more assertive and not afraid of confronting others. One of the reasons you are in therapy is to learn how to interact with others, and the therapy room is like a little laboratory where you can practice these skills.
2. You will probably learn something about yourself in the process of talking this over with the therapist.
3. You will learn that you can do something difficult, such as being more assertive.
4. You will also clarify in your own mind, through the help of the therapist, just what is bothering you and why you want to leave:
   • Perhaps you are running away from difficult issues that you are discussing;
   • Perhaps you are frustrated by the slow pace of therapy;
   • Perhaps the therapist isn't being as active as you'd like in the sessions.

After discussing your feelings you may feel better about continuing, or you and your therapist may agree that it is best for you to "terminate"—as ending therapy is called.

If you wish to continue in therapy, but find a new therapist, you can do so. Perhaps your present therapist will even help you find someone else. Or you can use the resources discussed elsewhere in this book.

MAINTAINING BOUNDARIES IN THERAPY: SEXUAL INTIMACY

One reason you would want to change therapists is if you think that something unethical or not right is going on. Crossing boundaries is one of these situations. Some therapists may hug or hold a patient if the person is very upset. But most therapists do not touch their patients at all. If you don't want to be touched, *say so,* and if the therapist objects, get a new therapist. This is especially true if the therapist touches you in any way that is sexual. You may talk about sexual feelings in therapy, but sexual touching or sexual actions of any kind are out of bounds. You may have sexual feelings toward someone that you want to discuss with your therapist. That is okay and is an important part of therapy. You may even have sexual feelings or feelings of love for your therapist. That is okay too, and you can tell your therapist about such feelings.

The purpose of bringing feelings up in therapy is to help you understand your needs and feelings toward others. But it can be very hurtful for you to act these out with your therapist, and an ethical therapist knows this. Don't sit on your therapist's lap, or let your therapist kiss you, or touch you in any way that doesn't feel quite right to you. It may make you feel special, and you may actually like the attention. But patients who have had intimate experiences with their therapists usually end up getting hurt. Eventually they feel betrayed by the person to whom they have turned to for help. They come to realize that they have been meeting the needs of the therapist instead of the other way around. Such behavior on the part of the therapist is unethical and may even be illegal, and it can only be harmful in the long run.

The vast majority of therapists do not cross these boundaries. It is brought up here as a warning. Be sure to tell someone if such a thing should happen so that the therapist can get help and no one else will be subjected to unethical behavior. You can tell your parents or the person who referred you to the therapist. You can report such behavior to the state or national professional association.

ENDING THERAPY

If you think that you have solved your problems or that you now feel better than before, you may decide that it is time for you to discontinue or terminate your therapy—at least for now. You know that you can always begin again, if you need to. It is good for you to discuss the ending of therapy with your therapist.

Often the therapist will suggest that you pick an ending date a few weeks away. In that way, you and the therapist can have time to say goodbye to each other and settle other issues of separation.

Sometimes patients end therapy abruptly, having difficulty ending relationships and saying goodbye. In their outside life, they do the same: just walk away from people. That is one reason that it is good to learn to take your leave in an informed way, so you can learn new behaviors that will help you in life.

Also, it is good to review how you have progressed and what issues may still remain for you to work on. It does not mean that you have to continue working on them now, but it is good for you to know what they are and how you can deal with them should they become problems when you are no longer in therapy.

If Your Therapist Suggests Ending Therapy

Your therapist may actually be the one who suggests that you terminate therapy. In such a case you may feel rejected. You may think that he can no longer help you or no longer wants to work with you. But the therapist may feel that the work you have set out to do has been accomplished, or that someone else with a different expertise may be a better person to treat you.

Again, it is important for you to discuss your feelings about the suggestion to terminate therapy. It may be hard to do, but it is important for you to understand the reasoning and your own reactions so that you do not leave these issues unresolved, buried and simmering inside you. If you feel angry or hurt, say so. If you are worried about hurting your therapist's feelings, say so.

If Your Parents Want You to Quit Therapy

It may be your parents who decide that you should discontinue therapy. Perhaps it is costing too much money, or perhaps you have been having arguments with them and they tell you that they don't think therapy is helping you. They may really believe that, and like many parents, they may underestimate how therapy works. They may not realize that it is a gradual process, and they may not notice changes in your behavior right away. And they certainly don't know what is going on inside you, how you are beginning to feel.

Some of your behavior that they find upsetting may simply be natural behavior for someone your age, as you learn to separate and grow up. But since you are in therapy, they may expect that you should not exhibit moodiness or other disrupting behaviors at home. On the other hand the therapy itself, in bringing up disturbing things, may cause you to act out at home. You may be feeling upset about what you are talking about, you may be feeling angry with your parents about things that they have done to you in the past that you are now discussing in therapy.

If your parents wish for you to discontinue therapy and you don't feel that you are ready, you should discuss this with your therapist. She may want to speak with them to explain what is going on; or if it is financial problems, she may be able to make other arrangements for you, such as reducing your fee or referring you to a low-cost clinic. Or your therapist may give you suggestions on how to talk to your parents about your wish to continue therapy. You may need to tell them that you are talking about things in therapy that upset you at times, that this is natural, and that you are trying to work these things out in therapy.

Your parents may want to know what you are talking about in therapy, and they may be particularly upset if they think you are talking about them. That may be a reason they would like you to quit, even though they may have been in favor in the first place. They now feel that someone else is getting too close to family secrets and may feel that they are bad parents. This is another reason it may be important for them to speak to your therapist.

Gina

Ever since Gina was a little girl she had been exposed to photographs of sexy-looking ladies: calendars hanging on the wall of her father's work-room, *Playboy* magazines lying around the living room. Her father's friends would come over, and she would hear them laughing and drinking beer, talking about women they had seen. Her mother on the other hand was a very plain woman, who dressed mostly in slacks and bagging sweaters and wore no lipstick or makeup at all. Despite this, the house was charged with sexuality, as a result of her father's behavior.

When Gina became a teenager, she began wearing tight-fitting clothes and wore very bright lipstick and heavy eye makeup, even to school. She got a lot of attention from the boys, and found herself becoming sexually active with them. At time she wasn't sure if that was what she wanted, yet it seemed like the only way to be. What upset her, though, was that her friendships or relationships with these boys were usually brief. So she found herself giving more and more to them, doing things with them that she didn't like to do, giving them gifts, and always being available to them hoping to be loved.

Then one day, Gina felt very uncomfortable near her vagina. She saw what looked like a sore or a bruise. It was quite painful. A visit to the doctor confirmed that she had contracted a herpes infection. She was only 16 years old. Gina felt devastated. She felt dirty, used, that her life was over. Who would ever want her now? She thought of killing herself, and she stayed in her room and cried and cried.

Gina's mother knew about the herpes infection. Both she and Gina had been told that it had come through sexual intercourse with someone who had it. It was the kind of condition that would stay in your body and Gina could expect outbreaks every once in a while. The doctor explained that the outbreaks would probably become less and less as time went by, but that she could give the virus to another

person if she had sex when she was having an out-
break. Just feeling that this virus was lurking in her
body, and that she could give it to someone else,
drove Gina to despair.

Her mother in desperation checked with her
health insurance company and got a list of psychotherapists who were providers for the company.
She picked out a name of a psychologist who had an
office near their home and called. She set up an
appointment for Gina.

Gina went to see the therapist, and cried and cried
through her sessions. She was at first hesitant, however, to tell the therapist about her behavior that had
led up to the infection. She was not sure how the
therapist would react. But in time she did start
talking about her relationships with others, and how
she felt about herself. And in time she talked about
her family and about the attitudes toward women and
girls that she had learned looking at those pictures.
She also remembered some of the men who had
come to visit her father and how they had looked
at her, particularly as she grew older. She began
resenting any man looking at her. And she began to
feel very angry, angry at her parents for not protecting her from this as a child. Angry at the boys who
had used her vulnerability. Yet she also realized that
she had been the one to make these choices.

One day after she had been in therapy for a few
months, she went into a rage at home. Her grandfather had been visiting, and he and her father had
gone out for the evening. The next day, her grandfather was laughing about the good time they had
had: They had gone to a topless bar. Gina was
shocked. She had never thought that her kindly

grandfather, this old man, could ever think like that, feel like that. "I could have been one of those young girls up there dancing," she said. "Is this what he thinks of me? I can't bear to let him touch me again, even to kiss me on the cheek. How can I ever feel safe again?" In her anger, she screamed at her grandfather and ran into her room, locking the door behind her. She refused to speak to anyone in the family for days.

In tears, Gina called her therapist from a pay phone. They got together the very next day. Gina was doubly upset, as her parents were now threatening to stop paying for her therapy. They felt that her behavior showed that she had not gained anything from all the money they had been paying.

They were unaware that the experiences Gina had had growing up at home had contributed to her behavior. They were also unaware that she was now beginning to understand her conflicts regarding her sexuality and her feelings toward her family. Perhaps they should have understood this, but both of her parents had grown up in families where sex was out in the open and women were seen as either "good girls" or "bad girls." And anyway Gina had never before reacted so violently to these behaviors on their part.

What they failed to realize was that as she was getting older and becoming a woman she was beginning to feel differently about herself and her body. And in therapy she was beginning to understand that, although her parents may have meant her no harm, they had exposed her to attitudes and stimuli that had led her to believe on some level that sex was the only way to be accepted, and that being sexy was the way women should be. But she was too young to understand how to be sexual and also to protect herself.

She had become overwhelmed with these feelings and the feeling of betrayal by her grandfather, when she felt that he was no different from all the others that she had trusted and been hurt by.

The case study of Gina shows how the effects of psychotherapy can be misunderstood by the family. It also shows how difficult it can be to talk about problems in your life. Yet over time, understanding and change are possible.

Eventually through therapy Gina was able to talk to her parents about what had been bothering her. Although they minimized their role, they apparently took what she said to heart. Their own behavior became more subdued over time, and the photographs and magazines began to disappear from the home. Through therapy, Gina learned to communicate with her parents, to accept herself, and to like herself.

She also came to terms with the herpes infection, as she realized that it didn't happen all the time and that many people have it—even nice people. She even came to consider it a kind of lucky event, something that had stopped her in her tracks and helped her to see that maybe she had better rethink her risky behavior. She began concentrating on her studies and making something of herself. And she began looking for relationships with boys who were more serious and fun-loving and who respected her.

CHAPTER 10

What Happens
in Sessions?

GETTING STARTED: MAKING THE APPOINTMENT

When you find the name of a therapist that you think you might like to talk to, phone to set up an appointment. If someone has referred you to the therapist, you can say so at this time. Should you get an answering machine or an answering service, leave your name and phone number, and give several times when you will be available for the therapist to call you back.

When you do speak to the therapist, ask the location of the office and the cost for the first visit.

If the office is in a convenient location and the fee does not seem impossible, set up an appointment.

First Phone Conversation

"Hello, this is (give your name)"

"I was referred to you by.............." (or, "I got your name from.............."

"I am interested in meeting with you for a consultation about my entering therapy with you."

"Could you tell me where your office is?"

"Could you give me an idea of your fee per session?"

"Do you have a sliding scale?"

Some therapists do not like to discuss fees over the phone. They prefer to meet with you and spend some time getting an understanding of your financial situation. If they have a "sliding scale," they can adjust your fee accordingly. If the therapist doesn't want to discuss fees over the phone, then you should ask:

"How much would the first consultation or meeting cost?"

If the therapist seems to be too expensive, you may ask him or her to suggest someone else or a clinic where low-cost therapy is available.

The Involvement of Parents

If you are under the legal age, it is likely that the therapist will want to speak with at least one of your parents. Many therapists want a parent to come with you to the first session and to some of the other sessions as well. This is partly for legal reasons, but also when children are still living at home their problems and the solution to their problems become family matters. For therapy to be successful, it requires cooperation and understanding from both sides: parents and children.

Therapists differ in their approach. Some may see you at times with your parents or parent, and at other times you separately and your parents separately. If you are over the legal age, your parents need not be involved at all.

THE FIRST SESSION

When you go for your first visit you will naturally be a bit nervous, particularly if you have never done anything like this. Leave enough time to get to your session, so you will not be late. Psychotherapy sessions begin right on time and end right on time. If you are late, you will lose time that is valuable to you.

What the Therapist May Ask You

During the first session the therapist will ask you some personal questions about yourself; questions about your . . .

- background
- family
- habits
- school
- friends

and most important,

- why you are there.

The therapist will want to know why you think you need therapy or counseling. If you completed the self-quiz in Chapter 2, you may want to refer to the items that you checked. Or you can just explain in your own words what is troubling you.

Try not to worry what the therapist will think of you as you are speaking; be as open and honest as you can. If you are nervous or concerned about the therapist's attitude toward you and your problems, say so, as that is also something very much worth talking about.

The first one to three sessions are usually used by the therapist as evaluation sessions, to help the therapist better understand you and to decide what treatment approaches are the best.

You too can use these first sessions as consultations, to see if you are comfortable with the therapist and to see if this is the person you would like to continue talking to for your therapy.

Sometimes it is difficult on the first visit to know if this is the person for you. So that is why two or three visits may be necessary.

If you do wish to come again, say so and make arrangements for the next appointment. If not, and if you feel comfortable doing so, you may tell the therapist that you do not wish to come again, or that you wish to think about it and will call back. Sometimes it is good to discuss your reservations about the therapist or therapy at this time. Your fears or concerns may be part of your hesitancy to undertake this new venture.

You may also want to have a discussion with your parents or someone else before committing yourself. That is okay. Just try to be sure that you are not just making excuses to get yourself out of something that you are a bit scared to do.

Sometimes people get the names of more than one therapist and visit two or three before making up their minds. Others find this confusing and prefer to see just one, and if that one does not work out, then look for another. Both approaches are acceptable.

Questions You Need to Ask the Therapist

Use this first session to interview the therapist. Feel free to ask the therapist's policies regarding:

- Paying for therapy
- Changing or canceling appointments
- The therapist's qualifications

These issues are discussed below and in other chapters.

PAYING FOR THERAPY

Psychotherapy can be costly, but it may be worth it if you consider it an investment in your life, your future.

Think through your budget as best you can, and discuss it with the therapist. If you don't think you can afford it, say so. If nothing can be worked out, ask for a referral to another therapist or a low-cost clinic.

If your mother or father will be paying for your sessions, find out how this is to be arranged, i.e., when and where a check should be sent.

Find out whether you are to pay at each session or at the end of the month.

Insurance

If you have insurance coverage, find out how the insurance forms are to be submitted and how the therapist wants to handle the payments. Find out if:

- you are to pay part of the fee and the insurance company the other part,
- the therapist will accept payments directly from the insurance company,
- the therapist expects you to pay the fee and then have the insurance company reimburse you.

If you think that one of your parents has insurance coverage, discuss this with them, if possible before going to see the therapist, so you will have the information that you need at the first visit.

For more information on paying for therapy see Chapter 11.

CHANGING OR CANCELING APPOINTMENTS

Find out how flexible the appointment schedule can be. What if you need to change your appointment time? Will you be able to reschedule? What happens if you need to cancel? How much notice do you need to give so you won't have to pay for the sessions.

Most therapists charge for a session if you don't show up, particularly if you don't let them know ahead of time. Some require that you notify them twenty-four hours in advance to avoid being charged. Others expect you to keep all appointments no matter what. There are many variations, so find out right away.

If you know ahead of time that you won't be able to keep an appointment, try to see if the therapist can reschedule you at another time. That will mean that you won't miss any sessions and perhaps that you won't have to pay for the missed session. If for some reason you have missed your appointment and didn't call ahead, leave a message acknowledging this and confirming that you will be there for the next appointment, or see if you can reschedule.

When you are late, remember that the hour that is held for you is *your* hour. If you are late, you are only cheating yourself. The therapy ends at a fixed time, after 45 or 50 minutes, depending upon the length of your sessions. If you are late, you just lose that time; sessions don't run over. If you know that you may be late, let the therapist know as soon as possible, so maybe something can be worked out.

EVALUATING THE THERAPIST

The Therapist's Qualifications

Don't be afraid to ask a professional about his qualifications, whether you are going to see the person privately or in a clinic. Although degrees and training do not guarantee that the person is skilled or right for you, knowing about background can give you some confidence that the person is qualified to help you. Anyone who has good qualifications will be proud to tell you and will respect you for trying to get the best help you can.

Your Comfort Level

After the first session, ask yourself how you felt about the therapist.

What was it like to talk to this person about the problems that are troubling you?

Did you hold anything back? You probably did. Most people reveal themselves only gradually.

Did you have a sense that the therapist was listening to you and understanding your feelings?

Is this someone that you trust?

Do you like the office location and setting?

Were you comfortable?

Will you be able to afford the fees?

If it doesn't feel right, pay for the first visit and go on to find someone else. If the chemistry does feel right to you and the practical matters can be worked out, then you can set up an appointment for the next visit.

Someone you feel comfortable working with, who can understand your problems and help you to overcome them is the kind of therapist you are looking for.

As part of your evaluation of your therapist and therapy, it is necessary for you to understand the process of therapy and the special therapeutic relationship that you will have with the therapist.

A SPECIAL KIND OF RELATIONSHIP

Your therapist is not exactly like a friend, not exactly like a teacher, and not exactly like a parent. Yet there are elements of each of these in the psychotherapeutic process.

Psychotherapy is a special kind of relationship. Sometimes the word *relationship* throws people, having different meanings to different people. Some people think of a relationship as being very close, very intimate. It scares them to think that they might be expected to get close to someone, particularly this stranger. Yet indeed you will be telling your deepest thoughts and secrets to this person, so therapy has an intimate quality to it.

But the therapy setting is special. It has its limits and

its boundaries, and it is important for you to understand these for your own protection. Although therapists vary in terms of their own interpretations of these boundaries, most follow them rather strictly.

A Safe Place

The therapy setting is to be a safe place for you. Helping you is the focus. You talk about yourself. The time is yours. It may frustrate you not to know about your therapist's private life, yet that is one of the boundaries. You are not there to help the therapist or to spend time learning about him or her. You may have questions about the therapist, or thoughts or fantasies, and it is important to bring these up in sessions. The therapist will share as much with you as he or she thinks is helpful to your treatment.

When you are in therapy, you do not socialize with the therapist outside of the office. This special relationship stays safely within the office walls. You have friends in your life, and if you don't, through therapy you can try to learn how to have them.

You must be able to trust the therapist and feel safe. Therapy is a working relationship, it is a partnership in which you work together. The therapist's role is to help you to find out what is troubling you and learn how to do something about it.

As you continue in therapy it is important to be continually thinking about how your therapy is going and whether you are comfortable with the therapist. It is usually good to discuss any reservations or feelings of discomfort that you have with the therapist. In the process you may learn something about your relationships with other people in your life.

THE PROCESS OF THERAPY

How your sessions proceed after the initial consultation depends in part upon what approach your therapist uses: psychodynamic, cognitive/behavior, or family therapy.

Psychodynamic Psychotherapy

In the more dynamic therapy, as discussed in Chapters 6 and 7, you will be expected to do most of the talking. It may be hard at first, as you don't really know this person. You may be hesitant to tell him certain things about yourself. Perhaps you are embarrassed or afraid he will think badly of you. Perhaps you are afraid others will find out what you are talking about, or that you will be punished once someone learns your secrets.

The more open you can be with the therapist about what has happened to you, or what you are afraid of, or ashamed of, the more quickly you can be helped. But sometimes you may not even know what is bothering you. Or you may not be able to put your feelings into words. The therapist is trained to help you. By listening to you, by asking questions, by telling you what he thinks you may be saying or feeling about yourself or others, your therapist can help you understand what you are going through.

Talking about your problems can be difficult. It's not easy to talk about very personal parts of your life.

- Perhaps you hate someone close to you.
- Perhaps you have cheated in school.
- Perhaps you have done something sexual that frightens you or confuses you.
- Perhaps you are afraid of someone.

- Perhaps you don't feel good about yourself, or think that you will never amount to anything.

Tell the therapist these feelings. Give some examples of things that have happened to you that are related to these feelings.

You may be afraid that if you talk about some of these things you will start to cry. That's okay; in fact, it may be good for you to let out all that tension, to allow yourself to feel sad.

Maybe you feel very angry with someone. Let the therapist know. Sometimes you may even feel angry with the therapist. Maybe you don't like something the therapist said or did. Say so.

What goes on in the room between you and the therapist is a very important part of therapy, for it helps you to uncover feelings and behaviors that may influence you in your interactions with others in your life.

Some therapists, particularly those more psychoanalytically trained, won't say much during the sessions. They expect you to do most of the talking. That can be very frustrating. Discuss this with the therapist. If it continues to be a problem, perhaps you should see someone who interacts more with you.

Maybe you are feeling angry that you have been told to be in therapy and it wasn't your idea. You don't want to be there and you don't want to talk to this person. That's quite understandable. But if you just sit there and don't talk, you won't get anything out of it. You may think that you don't care if you get something out of therapy or not. Yet help is available to you. Even if you just tell the therapist how angry you are that you have to be there, you may begin to feel better about having done just that.

Some therapists may play games with you; by that, I mean real games, such as Monopoly or cards. Through these games you can learn to relate to each other, and the therapist can learn about you: how you handle success, failure, frustration. You may be asked to draw pictures or do other activities. This may be a way to help you get into therapy and to become more comfortable with the therapist and the process. These activities also allow the therapist to see how you see the world and your place in it.

Defenses

Although you were the one who wanted to go into therapy, you may still have some resistance to the idea. You may not even be aware of the resistance. Psychologically, we try to protect ourselves from emotional upset and painful experiences. The way we customarily try to do that is through *psychological defenses.*

You use psychological defenses every day, just to get through life. For example, we try not to think too much about things that bother us, making ourselves get on with life. But when we are overwhelmed, our defenses don't work too well. We begin to feel all the sadness and anxiety that the defenses had tried to protect us from.

In therapy these defenses will still be working, and as the therapist tries to help you to talk about your life, you may find yourself avoiding subjects that trouble you, or you may find yourself getting angry with the therapist. Perhaps you will even deny that anything is wrong.

Denial is one of the major defenses; that is, not admitting to yourself that anything has happened or that something is wrong.

Avoidance is another defense. You start missing therapy sessions, always having what sounds like a good excuse. Or you start being late for sessions. Both of these defenses make it possible for you to avoid facing your problems.

Regression is acting the way you did when you were much younger. Perhaps you start to cry or act sick or use baby talk. It is a defense that gets you attention and gets you away from something threatening or unpleasant. But this behavior may make it hard for you to make friends or develop into a mature person.

Repression is pushing something out of your conscious mind. You may do it purposely; the experience may have been so unpleasant that the only way you can deal with it is to repress it. You say, "Well, why not just let it be." Sometimes that is a good approach, but not always. Just because you are not aware of something does not mean that it does not affect you. Memories that have been repressed can still be active in the unconscious memory. You may find yourself becoming anxious in certain situations, for example, and not know why. If the bad experience happened when you were quite young, it may not be remembered, but the uncomfortable feelings may surface now and you can't understand them. In therapy, these repressed feelings have a safe place in which to emerge and be understood. By doing so, you then gain control. You understand that your feelings are normal. You gain more control over your behavior as it is not controlled by feelings that you do not understand.

Identification with the aggressor is a defense that teenagers use a lot. An example is acting tough. To the world you present this tough, "I don't care" attitude, but it is a way of keeping people away from you.

Heather

Heather was fifteen when she started to dress punk and also when she got her first tattoo. She began going to heavy-metal concerts and clubs where everyone dressed in the latest mode, pins in their faces, lots of tattoos, and lots of leather. It was mostly the males who dressed this way, but Heather had outdone everyone. By the time she was nineteen, she had cut her hair real short, pierced her nose, and had large tattoos on her thighs and back.

Heather had been sexually molested when she was quite young. She had also lived with many foster families and had never really felt that she was safe. When she entered her teenage years, she felt insecure, vulnerable. Although she was now back living with her parents, they were both alcoholics. She felt that she was not safe anywhere or welcome anywhere.

By being part of the heavy metal scene, she felt that she gained some kind of identity. Younger teenagers looked up to her. People on the street noticed her, although inside it hurt when they made critical comments about her appearance. She looked very much like a tough man. In psychological terms, she had identified with her aggressor.

Afraid to trust people, particularly men, she took on many of their characteristics. The message was that she was tough and could handle herself. But the truth was otherwise. Her last boyfriend was the toughest of them all. Maybe he could protect her too. She also thought he was like her: someone who had suffered in life and was really good inside. But he too abused her sexually. Her defense had not worked.

Now in therapy, Heather was trying to get her life back into order. It was not easy. She had never thought the day would come when she would be nineteen and having to look forward to a job, or college, or marriage. But she had strengths, and her therapist recognized them. Together they slowly began the process of helping her deal with her past, her feelings about herself and others. Step by step she was learning to become the person she could be.

Not all defenses are bad. It's when they don't help us solve our problems or when they start to create new problems for us that defenses become harmful. In psychodynamic psychotherapy, you learn to analyze your defenses: Retain those that keep you emotionally healthy and change those that get in the way of your personal growth.

Cognitive or Behavioral Therapy

If you are in therapy for problem behavior in school, for example, your therapist may use cognitive or behavioral techniques. You may be asked to identify the situations where you get into trouble. Then you and the therapist may try out different ways that you could have responded. The next step would be for you to try these new ways of behaving in the school setting.

Other school-related problems that may be helped by cognitive or behavioral therapy are:

- anxiety at having to take tests, write papers, or speak up in class
- fear of failure or of not performing well
- procrastination or failing to get work done
- trouble getting along with classmates or teachers

- panic at flunking a test or getting a bad grade
- lack of direction or sense of purpose.

To help you with these adjustment problems, you may be asked to identify self-defeating ways of thinking about the demands of school. Then you will learn to think of ways in which you can change your behavior or your thoughts. You may be given "homework assignments" to do, exercises or suggestions of ways to behave in certain situations: You try out these new behaviors and then discuss what happened in the next session. Techniques used in this therapy are discussed in more detail in an earlier chapter.

Family Therapy

In family therapy, your parents go to the therapist with you. Sometimes you may go alone, as well. The basic idea is to help you communicate with your parents, and to help your family as a unit get along together. Although you may be the "identified patient," the family therapist realizes that your problems may be part of a larger family problem. In family therapy your parents may be asked to join with you in learning new ways of getting along.

Family therapy is conducted in a variety of ways. Sometimes you are given special assignments, exercises to do outside the office. These could include having each person in the family do something special for the others during the week. In the next session you discuss how it felt to do these special things, and whether it had any effect on how you are getting along with each other.

Each of the examples above are a small part of what might go on in therapy. They are mentioned only to give you an idea of the different ways therapy can be conducted. Basically, it is an experience and a process that takes place over time; it depends a great deal on the special relationship that you have with the therapist.

CHAPTER 11

How Can I Pay for
Therapy?

PRACTICAL AND PSYCHOLOGICAL ISSUES

If you are a minor and still dependent upon your parents
financially, you will probably need their cooperation in
paying for your therapy. In addition to the practical problems this may pose, there are also psychological issues
that get stirred up when children go into therapy.

Donald

Donald had been advised by his school counselor
that he needed psychotherapy. But Donald felt so
guilty. He knew that his family didn't have much
money and that they had a lot of expenses. Now this.
He was afraid to discuss it with his parents; they had
enough to worry about. And he knew they just
couldn't pay for it. Basically Donald was scared to
go into therapy: "Maybe I don't really need it," he
would say to himself.

Jill

Jill never felt that her mother took her problems seriously. If her mother was willing to pay for her therapy, she thought, that would show how much her mother cared. If she balked at the idea, then Jill would know she was right: No one really cared. And anyway, she said to herself, it was her parents' fault that her life was so difficult, so why not make them pay for it—in a big way.

Shawn

Shawn was hesitant to ask his parents to pay for his therapy. He wanted his sessions to be just between him and the therapist, and he knew that if his parents paid, they would want to know they were getting their money's worth. He was afraid they would "butt in"—that they would want to know what he was saying to the therapist, and that they might say the wrong things to the therapist, turning the therapist against him.

He also worried that if his father got involved, he would mess everything up. His father was a strong person and very argumentative. Shawn was afraid the therapist wouldn't like his father and might not be strong enough to stand up to him. He was also afraid that the therapist wouldn't like Shawn anymore after dealing with his family. And if his parents got involved in paying for therapy, couldn't they just end it when they felt like it—sort of like a punishment for him if he didn't do what they wanted him to do. By paying for his therapy, his parents would have control over him again, just as they always seemed to have control over his life.

Carol

Carol's parents always gave her everything she wanted—everything material, that is. They constantly bought her gifts, gave her money to buy clothes, let her go to the movies no matter how much it cost. But she felt they were really never there for her, that the presents were just to buy her love. Her parents never spent any time with her and were very cold emotionally. Sure, she knew they'd pay for therapy, just like they paid for everything else. Somehow it didn't feel right. She wanted this to be *her* therapy, something that she was doing for herself.

Discussing Money with Your Therapist

You may feel uncomfortable talking to the therapist about payments. Perhaps you don't want her to know that your parents don't have enough money. You don't want to feel like a "charity case." Maybe you're afraid that your mom will try to bargain your therapist down in his fee—and that would embarrass you.

On the other hand, you may want your new therapist to be impressed by the fact that your dad makes a lot of money. At the same time, you may want to protect your father, so that people won't try to take advantage of him (or you) and try to get his (or your) money.

More than likely, though, you are like most young people who really are not sure how much money your parents have. One moment they are talking about how tight things are and that you can't have this or that, and the very next day they are buying a new car or offering to take you on a vacation. And if your parents are divorced, you may be hesitant to be in the middle again of all the arguing over money: Who's supposed to pay for this and who won't pay for that?

These are all issues that need to be discussed with your therapist and with your parents as well. They are very legitimate issues for discussion in therapy, even after the fee has been agreed upon. Money issues follow us throughout life and often are symbolic of how we feel about ourselves and others. Money means different things to different people—and sometimes several things at once. Money can represent power, independence, caring, self-worth, control, dependency, generosity, love.

An Investment in Your Future

Therapy is like an investment, an investment in yourself, your life. You may feel that you need to move on, to change things, to learn to handle problems as they arise. Therapy can be costly, but there is usually a way to afford it once you are committed to going.

HOW MUCH DOES IT COST?

Therapists in Private Practice

Seeing a therapist in private practice is usually the most expensive way. You may wonder why someone would choose this route over a clinic, if it's more expensive. One reason is that in a clinic you may not be able to choose your therapist. (You usually can ask for a change, however, if you don't like the person to whom you are assigned.)

Because therapy fees are fairly high and you may need to see the therapist for a considerable period of time (e.g., once or twice a week for months or years), the costs need to be figured into your family's budget.

The cost of therapy varies depending on where you live. The most costly places are cities, particularly in the Northeast. The least costly are in the Midwest. Most therapists have a sliding scale, which means that they will give you a slightly lower fee if you can't afford their full fee. That's one reason they will need to speak to your parents, so they can understand your family's income and financial responsibilities.

The following chart gives you an idea of the average fees charged. (Since this is an average, some of these therapists will charge a bit more than this range, others a bit less.)

Average Range of Fees

Therapist	Per session
Psychiatrists	$100–$125
Psychologists	$85–$100
Social Workers	$50–$75
Other counselors	$40–$65

It is not necessarily true that the higher the fee, the better the therapist. Although more experienced people usually are more expensive, sometimes those just starting out in practice charge high fees to make people think that they are good.

In general, psychiatrists are the most expensive and social workers and counselors the least. In our culture, physicians have high social status and thus are able to command higher fees. They are the professionals who prescribe medication and who also treat the more severely disturbed patients; in these instances, they have increased responsibilities.

Psychologists on the other hand usually have more extensive training in psychotherapy than the other mental health professionals. That accounts in part for their relatively high fees.

Therapists who are not state licensed may charge quite low fees, so beware if it sounds like too much of a bargain (unless it is a subsidized mental health clinic).

Although important, cost is not the only reason to choose a particular therapist. You need to find someone who is experienced, qualified, and right for you. Then see how you can arrange to pay. Later in the chapter we discuss the various ways of paying for therapy.

In addition to therapists in private practice, there are also low-cost clinics in most communities.

Community Mental Health Centers

These centers are staffed by mental health professionals and are supported by either the federal, state, or local government. The fees are set according to your ability to pay. Such centers are listed in the Yellow Pages of the telephone directory, either under Mental Health Centers, Mental Health Clinics, or the state Department of Mental Health. You can also find out about them by talking to your parents or school counselors.

Hospital and University Mental Health Clinics

Hospitals often have mental health clinics that are operated by the Department of Psychology or Psychiatry.

Call the local hospital to find out. Fees are usually adjusted to meet your ability to pay, and insurance is usually accepted.

Many universities have mental health clinics staffed by therapists in training. These therapists are supervised by experienced and licensed therapists. You can find out if one exists in your community by calling the Psychology Department of a local university or college.

College Student Counseling Centers

If you are in college or planning to go to college, you may choose to see someone in the Student Counseling or Student Mental Health Center. These services usually are free, but may be limited to a given number of sessions. If it appears that you would benefit from longer-term therapy, or if your situation requires more intensive therapy, they will help you make arrangements to be seen privately or at a mental health clinic.

METHODS OF PAYING FOR PSYCHOTHERAPY

Parents Paying Full Fee

Your parents may prefer to pay your full fee and may be able to do so. However, since therapy is costly, most parents will look for other means to help them cover at least part of the expense.

Health Insurance

You may be covered by either your mother's or your father's health insurance. If they are working, more than likely they have group coverage through the place where they work. Unfortunately, insurance coverage for medical illnesses is usually better than that for psychological problems. Sometimes patients need only pay a few dollars as a copayment for medical care but will have to pay a much larger amount for mental health care.

For example, one common kind of coverage pays up to 50 percent per medical session, but only up to $40 per mental health session. But you see from the chart that most private therapists' fees are much more than $40. So actually you would be reimbursed only $20 on this policy (that is 50 percent of $40 = $20). You or your parents would have to make up the difference.

If the therapist charges $90 per session, you would have to pay the additional $70 ($20 + $70 = $90).

A better policy might reimburse 80 percent of the fee no matter what the fee is. In this case the insurance company would pay $72 (80 percent of $90 = $72), and you would only have to pay the difference of $18 ($72 + $18 = $90).

Not only do policies differ in the percentage or amount they pay per session, but they may also have limits ("caps") on how much they will cover per year or for your lifetime. And there are usually deductibles, which means that you may have to pay the first $100 or $200 each year.

Most insurance gives you coverage as an *inpatient*, that is, if you have to be hospitalized for a psychiatric illness. But not all insurance covers you if you are seeing the therapist as an *outpatient* in a private office. It is important that your parents speak to their insurance company to be sure just what is covered for *outpatient psychotherapy*. The government is going to be making changes in health coverage laws in the years to come, and hopefully the coverage for psychological needs will improve.

Health Maintenance Organizations

Managed health care is a new form of insurance that is becoming more popular. If you or your family belong to a Health Maintenance Organization, the HMO usually has a center where you can be treated by their own professionals, with the HMO paying all or a percentage of the fee. In this case you do not always get to choose your own therapist, but must use one of their providers. Sometimes you can make arrangements to use someone outside the system, but the amount reimbursed will be less.

Another variation of this is the Preferred Professional Organization (PPO). In this case, you can choose a professional from a list. You can see the therapist in his or her private office, and the fee and manner of payment would be set by the PPO, according to your policy.

HMOs and PPOs differ in their plans and payments; if that is the coverage that your family has, you would have to investigate how it can be used in your case.

Medicaid

If your family's income is not high, you may qualify for the federal-state financial aid program called Medicaid. Your parents can find out about this program at the welfare office in your community. If your family qualifies for Medicaid, your psychotherapy will be paid for by Medicaid. Although you can choose your own therapist, he or she must be on the list of "qualified Medicaid providers." Many therapists do not choose to be on this list, because of the enormous amount of paperwork required and other inconveniences related to the government bureaucracy. Also, Medicaid sets the fee that the therapist is allowed to charge, which is usually much less than what therapists in the area charge. Your local Medicaid office, however, should be able to give you the names of providers in your area.

CHAMPUS

You may be covered for psychotherapy if one of your parents is in the armed forces (i.e., federal government uniformed service personnel). The health insurance that covers dependents is known by the acronym CHAMPUS. This plan currently pays 20 to 25 percent of the fee for outpatient mental health services, after the deductible amount has been paid for by you. Most therapists accept this form of payment, as it usually bases its payments on the full fee, unlike Medicaid or other insurance programs that limit how much the therapist's fee may be.

Working to Pay for Your Own Therapy

In most of the options discussed above, only a portion of the cost of your therapy may be covered. Your parents may be able to help you with the remainder. However, it is important for you to consider paying for some or all of the remaining therapy costs yourself. This is something that you can discuss with your therapist.

There are psychological as well as practical advantages to working to pay for treatment. For one, by doing so you are making it "your own therapy." It is a way for you to become more independent, to feel that you have more control over the choices that affect your life. The therapy will seem to belong to you. If your parents are in a financial bind, you may be helping them out, and perhaps making sure that you will be able to have therapy. On the other hand, with school and your other responsibilities you may not have time to work. Some therapists suggest that young clients work even if the parents can pay, as a way of learning to assume more responsibility for their lives. It is something for you to think about seriously and to discuss with your therapist.

CHAPTER 12

Will Anyone Else Find Out?

When you first start therapy you may be hesitant to talk openly with the therapist. You are not sure how the therapist will judge you, and you wonder who else may find out about what goes on. In fact you may not even want anyone to know that you are in therapy.

You've heard kids making jokes about people being "weird" or "crazy." You're afraid they'll think the same of you, and even worse that they might publicly tease you or not want to be with you. Or maybe you know someone who is seeing a therapist or is in family therapy. You don't want to be like that person. You used to think that doing something like that was stupid or weak.

On the other hand, you may have wondered what actually goes on in therapy and at times even wished that you had someone you could talk to.

CONFIDENTIALITY AND TRUST

Therapy is based on trust. You need to feel free to speak openly to your therapist about anything. You may want to tell the therapist about:

- how bad you feel
- thoughts or actions that you are not proud of
- your feelings toward others, including parents, friends, teachers, and even the therapist herself.

But you wonder whether the therapist will tell anyone? Will anyone else find out?

What makes your relationship with your therapist different from many other relationships is this element of trust and confidentiality. By confidentiality, we mean that the therapist does not tell anyone what goes on in your sessions. Thus, you can feel free to talk about anything you want to talk about. But there are exceptions to this rule of confidentiality. In certain circumstances the therapist may need to let someone know about your therapy. We will discuss these circumstances below.

DIFFERENCES BETWEEN ADULTS AND MINORS

It is important that you discuss the issues of *confidentiality* with the therapist when you first meet, so you will know how they affect you. If you are a minor (that is, under the legal age for your state), different laws apply to you than to adults. The legal age when you become an adult differs from state to state, but is usually somewhere between sixteen and eighteen years of age.

WILL MY PARENTS HAVE TO KNOW?

If you are a minor, your parents or guardian may want to be involved in your therapy. In fact, in most instances a therapist will not see a minor without a parent's consent and unless a parent is involved in some way.

Your therapist may want to meet with you and your parents together and sometimes with your parents or a parent alone. Your parents may want to know periodically how you are doing and if there is anything that they can do to help you. As much as possible, your therapist will try to respect your privacy and not tell your parents your deepest secrets.

But there are times when it may be useful for your parents to know some things about you. Your therapist will help you to figure out how to tell them. The difficulty you may have talking to your parents about your problems or about something that has happened to you may be a signal that there is something more basically wrong in your relationship with them. By learning how to talk to your parents, you will be helping to open up communication with them.

Maybe you'd actually like someone to find out some of the things that you are telling the therapist. Maybe you want the therapist to tell your parents something that you are afraid or hesitant to tell them. You can of course give the therapist your permission to speak to them.

If you are of legal age, the therapist is supposed to keep anything that you say, do, or reveal in strictest confidence. The therapist is not even to tell anyone that you are in therapy, unless you give permission. The therapist can share information about you with others only when she has discussed this with you and has your consent, preferably in writing. However, there are some exceptions.

WHEN DO OTHERS NEED TO KNOW?

There may be times when your therapist needs to tell others about your case. In such situations you may give your permission and your therapist may ask for written consent.

Insurance Companies

One common area today where some information may need to be shared involves "third party payers," which are usually insurance companies or HMOs that pay your therapy bills. If you or your parents have coverage for psychotherapy, your therapist must fill out and sign the insurance form for you to receive the payment.

To keep costs down, many of these companies want to be sure that the therapy is necessary and that it is being helpful. They may request that your therapist periodically send them reports about your progress. To protect your confidentiality, in most cases the therapist will discuss your case in as general terms as possible: what your problem is (e.g., your diagnosis), the kind of treatment that is being provided, and how you are progressing. Sometimes the insurance company will want to know how your problems are affecting your schoolwork, your job, or your relationships with others. They also want data such as the dates of your sessions and cost.

Although insurance companies are also supposed to keep confidentiality, there is of course no guarantee. The papers go through the hands of many clerks, personnel officers, and other workers. Whether the fact that you were in therapy would ever affect you in the future, such as to jeopardize a job or a school situation, is remote but cannot be ruled out. Many people use insurance to pay for therapy, but if this is a concern of yours you may want to figure out how to pay for your therapy without using your insurance. You can discuss your concern with the therapist during your first session.

Professional Consultations

The therapist may ask your permission to talk with your previous therapist or counselor, if you have been in therapy before; or to speak to a medical doctor who has been treating you; a lawyer, if a legal issue is involved; or a probation officer if the therapy is court-mandated.

If you are being seen in a mental health clinic or a student counseling center at college, your case may be discussed in case conferences, or your therapist may confer with colleagues. The therapist may discuss your case with other therapists without your consent, if it is done for professional reasons. The therapist may want to get some advice about some aspect of your problem or the therapy itself. Ethically the therapist is supposed to discuss only information that is relevant to the specific issue being discussed, and the consultants or colleagues are obligated to keep the discussion confidential.

Sometimes the therapist is in training and will need to discuss your case with a supervisor and with other therapists in case conferences. In some cases, the therapist may ask permission to tape record your sessions. He may want to review your sessions for his own purposes or to play them for his supervisor. Ask the therapist what he plans to do with the recorded sessions. If you do not want them taped, say so. If taping is necessary for your being seen in that clinic or office, you can ask for a referral to someone who will not need to tape the sessions.

There is, by the way, a positive side to having professionals discuss your case. You get the benefit of the experience and ideas of more than one skilled person helping you. And in the case of those in training, they are supposed to be supervised by someone who is experienced.

WHEN OTHERS MUST BE TOLD

In some situations, state laws require the therapist to break confidentiality. These are instances where the information is considered to be in the "public good":

- The intention to harm or kill others
- Child abuse or neglect
- Risk of suicide or self-harm
- Loss of touch with reality: psychosis
- Intention to commit a crime
- Court-ordered evaluation or therapy.

The Intention to Harm or Kill Others

If you have indicated to the therapist that you intend to physically harm or kill someone, the therapist is obligated to protect that person. Therapists can warn the person or notify someone who will warn the threatened person. The therapist may also notify the police and, if necessary, may have you hospitalized.

Please understand that this does not mean that you cannot tell a therapist that you are mad at someone or even that you hate someone. You can even express a wish that someone were dead. We are talking here about the therapist's judgment that you actually plan to hurt someone else.

You might ask why someone would tell a therapist that they are going to do something violent. In doing so, they might be asking for the therapist's help; they might want the therapist to stop them.

Child Abuse or Neglect

When therapists learn about physical or sexual abuse of a minor, they are obligated to report it to the child welfare authorities in the state and in some instances to the police. This includes neglect that may be injurious to the child's health or welfare. It would apply to any abuse or neglect that you may have suffered as a child (now or in the past), or abuse or neglect of any child that you may know of. In some states, abuse and neglect of the elderly and those who are retarded must also be reported.

The purpose of these laws is to protect the child and other children who might be affected and to get help for the person who is responsible for these acts.

You may be afraid of what will happen to you and to others. You may be afraid that you will be hurt in some way, that your family will be broken up, that you may anger someone, get yourself into trouble, or start something that you cannot control. These are natural and realistic concerns. But the situation itself is usually worse than what happens when the authorities become involved. You need protection and the other person needs help.

You should discuss your concerns and fears with the therapist before going into details. Find out what the therapist intends to do with the information, what might happen as a result, and how it might affect you and others.

Risk of Suicide or Self-harm

If your therapist thinks that you really intend to kill yourself or hurt yourself, she must send you to a hospital where you will be safe and receive treatment. This does not mean that you can't tell your therapist how sad you are.

When people are depressed, they often have fantasies about killing themselves. They may think about how they would do it and how other people might react afterward. Sometimes when things seem out of control and you can't think of any other way out of your pain, you may think of hurting yourself. You can tell all of this to a therapist; in fact you should do so.

Just feeling so low and thinking about hurting yourself does not mean that you actually plan to do it. Sometimes merely telling someone can make you feel better. When you find that your therapist understands, it helps. Sometimes when people are very depressed, the therapist will prescribe medication for a while to help them over the depression. It may take a few weeks for the medication to have an effect, but it can be enormously helpful.

Your therapist does not have to tell anyone if you are having suicidal thoughts. She will first want to know how serious your thoughts are, if you really intend to hurt yourself. She may ask you to make a contract with her, promising that you will not hurt yourself while you and your therapist are working on your problems. She may ask you to call her when you are feeling particularly bad.

It is only when the therapist feels that you have an actual plan to kill yourself and that you plan to do so very soon, that she is obligated to take action. Most people have mixed feelings about killing themselves and feel much safer when their therapist takes their plan seriously and does something to stop them. When they then have had time to work on their problems, to learn how to take control of their lives, they are glad that they didn't do it.

You may have heard about someone who has committed suicide; maybe it was someone in your family or in your school. If it was someone in your family, you may feel sad and wish to join them. If it was someone in your school, you may be curious about what it was like those last minutes; you notice how others are upset about what happened and all the attention and love that comes from everyone. But you must remember that after the fact you won't know about others' reactions. You will be dead.

If you do feel this way or have felt this way, don't be afraid to speak to a therapist. Your therapist is a trained professional, someone who wants to understand your pain and to help you. It may take time. It may eventually involve others in your care, but it is certainly worth the try.

Loss of Touch with Reality: Psychosis

Sometimes people can be suffering from a mental illness and become out of touch with reality. They may hear voices telling them to kill someone, for example. They may become paranoid and feel that there is a conspiracy and that people are out to get them. These irrational thoughts can become very frightening and the person's judgment can become impaired.

Therapists are trained to evaluate people's emotional and mental states and to make clinical judgments about whether they may be dangerous to themselves or others. If the therapist feels that the person is psychotic, she may have to have the patient restrained or hospitalized for a while for treatment. In the hospital the patient will be in an environment where he or she can feel safe. The person can calm down and may be helped through medication and psychotherapy. Today usually hospitals do not confine patients for mental conditions too long. With the new medications, patients are out often in a matter of days or weeks. If the condition is a chronic one, the patient may need to stay on medication and under the supervision of a psychiatrist after discharge from the hospital.

Intention to Commit a Crime

In many states therapists must report to the police if they learn that a patient intends to commit a felony.

Court-ordered Evaluation or Therapy

When a person is ordered by a court to be examined by a psychologist or a psychiatrist, the therapist must file with the court a report on his findings.

A person may be ordered by the court to be in therapy as a condition of probation. The therapist then must keep the probation officer informed that the person is keeping appointments. Usually the contents of the sessions are not revealed.

IN SUMMARY

To sum up, basically the therapist's office is a safe place for you to share your innermost thoughts and fears and to work out your problems. We have mentioned some special cases in which the therapist may have to break the confidentiality, such as if you intend to harm yourself or others, or if you are psychotic and out of touch with reality. Usually the therapist will let you know when he or she needs to tell someone about your situation. In some instances the therapist will ask your permission to speak with others about you. In the vast majority of cases, however, *what you tell your therapist is just between the two of you, working together for your good.*

CHAPTER 13

What About Medication?

Sometimes a therapist may suggest that you take medication. At first this suggestion may be upsetting to you. You wonder:

- Does that mean that therapy isn't working?
- Does it mean that I'm crazy?
- Will I get addicted?
- What about side effects?
- Will I have to take it forever?
- Will it change me in some way that I won't like?

You are right to be concerned about medication. It is something that you should take seriously. Before you take any medication you need to understand:

- *Purpose*: Why you might take it,
- *Results*: What you can expect from it, and
- *Side Effects*: What you need to watch out for.

It is also important for you to know that thousands of people take medication for emotional problems and benefit from it. But it is not for everyone, which is why we want you to understand what is involved and why your therapist might think it could help you.

WHEN IS MEDICATION INDICATED?

Medication is often recommended when you are feeling depressed or anxious and your symptoms are very severe. You may also want to consider medication if you have felt depressed or anxious for a long time and you don't seem to be getting any better even though you have been in psychotherapy. You may have heard of antidepressants, such as Prozac, or antianxiety drugs, such as Valium. But there are many different kinds of medications, and new ones are being developed all the time.

Taking medication when you've been feeling down is similar to taking it when you have a medical or physical illness, such as a headache or other pain or discomfort. In fact, your body and your emotions are very much interrelated. For example, when you have been under stress for a long time your body uses up a lot of the chemicals that help it run efficiently. The medication helps the body to recover and to replenish these chemicals, getting your body back into balance. Medication may not be the first recommendation in the course of your treatment, but at some point it may be beneficial. After talking with you, your therapist may feel that you might benefit from taking medication along with your psychotherapy.

Johnny

Johnny was so depressed that he was not able to function in school. At home he just sat around, often staring out the window thinking of ways that he could kill himself. He knew that he wouldn't actually do that, but just thinking about it made him feel better. It was the only solution could think of—just disappearing. He was constantly getting into fights at school, and felt all alone. His parents had pretty much given up on him, as he wouldn't speak to them. He spent most of his time at home alone, looking at TV or just sleeping.

Johnny agreed to go to therapy, but when he met with the therapist, he barely spoke. He was angry, scared. He felt that if the therapist was so smart he could just tell him what to do. Deep inside, he felt no one could really help him, and even more no one cared. All this anger was draining his energy.

Johnny's therapist, Dr. Thomas, thought that antidepressant medication could help him, that in addition to being angry, he was suffering from depression. The medication would not make him feel "high" but would even out his moods so he wouldn't feel so out of control. They would continue to meet for therapy, but the medication would make it possible for Johnny to focus on the issues in his life that were bothering him. It would give him the energy to take charge.

Johnny was shocked when Dr. Thomas suggested medication to him. His first reaction was that his therapist thought he was crazy. Johnny's uncle had been on some kind of medication for years, and he had even been in hospitals for acting in bizarre ways. Johnny was scared. Would they put him in a hospital too?

His first response was no. He didn't even want to discuss it. But as the weeks went on, and he felt no better, he began to wonder if maybe Dr. Thomas's pills could help. But then he was afraid to ask. When Dr. Thomas brought it up again, Johnny listened. This time the therapist seemed to be more insistent, he thought. Maybe he could give it a try. But what would these drugs do to him? He knew kids at school who were addicts, taking drugs; would he become an addict?

But as he continued to feel so down and nothing seemed to be helping him, Johnny agreed to try medication. After the first few days of taking the pills he really didn't feel anything. He figured they weren't working. But as time went on he realized that he was feeling better, that he was going about his business at school and at home and not being so upset. He was almost acting like other kids. Johnny felt in a way like he had never felt before. Not really happy, but not so sad either. He was less angry and didn't seem to be getting into fights any more. He had more patience. Was it the medication? he asked himself. The therapy? Or was he just feeling better on his own?

Sometimes that is the way psychotropic medication works. It doesn't feel powerful, not like some street drug. Your doctor monitors it for you. It just evens out your moods, makes your behavior less impulsive, helps you to concentrate. Medication does not solve all your problems; you will probably still have to be in therapy. But you are now able to use your therapy better. Instead of focusing on those awful moods that just don't seem to go away, you can look at those things in your life that you can change, that you can do something about.

Most people who take medication for psychological

problems are adults. Although teenagers can often benefit from some of the same medications, they are used less frequently with young people, particularly elementary school-age children.

Some parents, however, do not want their children on any kind of medication and may urge you to hang on and give therapy a chance. You yourself may not like the idea of "putting chemicals" into your body. And in the course of weeks or months, you may actually begin to feel better without the medication.

However, it can happen that you are too disabled to wait weeks or months, and the psychiatrist may feel that there is no need to have you suffer when help through medication is available. This is something that you, your parents, and the doctor need to discuss together.

DEPRESSION

Depression is more than just feeling unhappy. Sometimes you may not even realize that you are depressed. Perhaps you have always felt that way, and so you think it is normal. However, you notice that others don't seem to feel or act the same way that you do.

How do I know if I'm depressed? Some common symptoms are:

- Having long-lasting feelings of sadness, helplessness, unworthiness, and guilt
- Not being able to feel pleasure
- Having mood swings, going frequently from feeling quite down to being very active, happy, or angry
- Being irritable and oversensitive
- Being self-critical

- Having low self-esteem
- Thinking about dying
- Not sleeping well—either having trouble falling asleep at night, or not being able to get up in the morning
- Not eating properly—having no appetite or eating too much, particularly junk food
- Daydreaming and not being able to concentrate
- Having a decline in your school performance
- Not being interested in being with your friends
- Having headaches, stomachaches, fatigue.

These are only some of the symptoms that may be indicative of depression. Remember that all of us at one time or another may have such feelings. It is when you have many of them and they don't seem to go away that you may be suffering from depression.

Young children are usually not given medication for depression. The symptoms and behaviors are usually worked out in psychotherapy, if they become serious enough. Teenagers and college students may be given antidepressant medication on the following indications:

- If they are suicidal
- If they are so withdrawn and depressed that they are unable to function
- If their behavior is disrupting their life and the process of therapy seems not fast enough.

What Causes Depression?

It is not always clear which comes first, the chicken or the egg, as the saying goes. Did something outside of our bodies cause us to feel bad and affect the chemical im-balance? Perhaps someone died, or perhaps you failed a course?

Or did the body's chemical balance get off first, making you feel bad. Chemicals in the brain, called *neuro-transmitters*, help in the sending of electrical impulses between nerve cells, making it possible for the brain to process information and regulate body activity.

In one sense we are all really machines that work by means of chemical reactions and electrical discharges. Sometimes the chemicals get out of balance, and this affects the way we feel and act. Like brakes in a car, for example, they may need to be readjusted. Since we can't go directly into the brain to make the repairs, we do the adjusting through other means: chemicals (pills) to regu-late the body, to change the chemical imbalance.

A biological depression is suspected when there is a family history of depression or when you have been de-pressed for a long time, for years perhaps. In such cases, a medical intervention that regulates your body chemistry may be what helps you to feel better.

Medication and Treatment for Depression

Before prescribing any medication, the psychiatrist ex-amines the person to make a thorough evaluation. In some cases, the evaluation will include laboratory tests, psycho-logical testing, and consultations with other specialists. In the case of depression, a class of drugs called *antidepres-sants* is used.

Antidepressants correct the imbalance of chemicals that act as the brain's messengers. The earliest type of antide-pressants was a class called: *monoamine oxidase inhibitors* (phenelzine/Nardil; tranylcypromine/Parnate, and others).

These were followed in 1957 by *tricyclics* (imipramine/ Tofranil; amitriptyline/Elavil, and others).

Both of these classes of drugs have some side effects: With MAO inhibitors, you may experience restlessness or afternoon sleepiness; with tricyclics you may experience drowsiness, a dry mouth, or a gain in weight. Although more serious side effects are not common, it is important to report to your doctor any changes in your body or mood.

The newest antidepressants are of a class called *selective serotonin reuptake inhibitors* (SSRIs), (e.g., Prozac and Zoloft). Serotonin is a mood-affecting chemical (*neurotransmitter*) that is released by neurons in the brain as part of the brain's normal activity. By blocking the neurons from reabsorbing and metabolizing serotonin after they release it, SSRIs increase the amount of serotonin available for the transmission of electrical impulses between the brain's neurons. For some reason not well understood, this process helps to relieve depression.

SSRIs have less troublesome side effects than tricyclics, but until you become adjusted to the medication you may experience some mild side effects such as restlessness, nervousness, sleepiness, or insomnia. Some people feel light-headed and describe feeling a bit "spacey." These side effects usually go away in a few days, but if they do not, tell your doctor and she can adjust the amount or kind of medication you are taking.

ANXIETY

Fears and anxieties are a normal part of growing up. Children may be afraid of the dark, of separating from their parents. Older children may become anxious over the demands of school, such as exams and grades. In high school, it is normal to be worried about being accepted by others and issues around sexuality.

It is when these concerns become excessive and unrealistic, when they interfere with your normal functioning, that therapy may be called for. When the worries begin to keep you from school, from being with others, from eating or sleeping, you may need professional help. Also if you frequently have physical problems, such as headaches and stomachaches, you may be under a lot of stress and feeling anxious. Teenagers and adults may be given medication if their symptoms are extremely disruptive to their lives.

Phobias, or extreme fears of certain objects, are also a form of anxiety. Perhaps you are terrified of dogs, or high places, or the dark. Often phobias can be treated quite well with behavioral therapy. But there are times when antianxiety medication can be helpful as well.

Another phobia or fear that can become immobilizing is the *fear of death or illness*. Such a reaction may be natural if you have been ill yourself, or if someone in your family has had a serious illness or died. But if this fear lasts for a long time and gets in the way of your life, you may need to seek professional help.

Panic attacks and other anxiety states are also common. Some people have sudden feelings of extreme terror or impending doom. Victims begin to sweat and their hearts beat madly. They become afraid that they are dying. If you suffer from panic attacks, you may find that they occur when you are in closed-in spaces, like elevators or crowded rooms, or when you are asked to speak in front of your class at school. Sometimes they may happen when you expect to be separated from your parents, either when you are going away or when they are going away. Just thinking about these kinds of situations can trigger an attack.

Medication and Treatment for Anxiety

Antianxiety medication in the form of benzodiazepines (alprazolam/Xanax and others) may be used when a person is highly anxious or having difficulty sleeping. A common side effect is drowsiness. Do not use alcohol when you are taking these drugs.

Sometimes antidepressants are used in the treatment of anxiety, particularly in the prevention and treatment of panic attacks. Again, medication for anxiety is used in conjunction with ongoing psychotherapy. You should continue to see the psychiatrist while you are on medication, so she can make whatever adjustments may be needed.

HYPERACTIVITY

Although it is normal for young people to have a lot of energy, there are those who are extremely active, who have difficulty concentrating and sitting still, and who act very impulsively. This behavior is referred to as hyperactivity, or technically *attention deficit hyperactivity disorder* (ADHD).

Persons with ADHD seem unable to control themselves and feel very edgy in their own bodies, particularly if they are in a situation where they can't move around. You may have seen people like this in school, or perhaps you recognize these behaviors and feelings in yourself.

Hyperactive kids talk a lot and get into problems with their teachers for acting out. They fidget and are easily distracted. They rarely finish what they start and always seem to be losing things. They have trouble listening and constantly interrupt others. They get into trouble for doing things that they have been told not to do. It is as if they cannot control themselves. Does this describe you or someone you know?

Medication and Treatment for Hyperactivity

The medications that are usually prescribed for hyperactivity are called *stimulants*, the most common of which is *Ritalin* (methylphenidate). This medication often must be taken every day and some parents object to that. However, when the medication has a positive effect, both the parents and the child are often relieved. Ritalin has usually been used with elementary age children, but some psychiatrists have found that it also works well for high school and college students.

You may wonder why someone who is very active would be given a "stimulant," since the word implies making people peppy. But with people who have ADHD, these medications seem to have the opposite effect: They help them to concentrate and feel more in control. Stimulants, however, do not work for all hyperactives, nor do they alleviate all symptoms.

ATTENTION DEFICIT DISORDER

A condition related to ADHD but that does not include hyperactivity is *attention deficit disorder* (ADD). Those with ADD typically have problems concentrating on their work. They may have reading problems as well. Thus, in school students with ADD do not do as well as they themselves or others might expect them to do. Their frustrations with school work may make them act out (such as being the class clown) or act impulsively. Some students with ADD become depressed, not understanding why they have to take so long and try so hard to do what others seem to do so easily. If you have ADD you may have low self-esteem and feel that you are "stupid." Yet you may be quite bright. ADD is what is called a "learning disability." (See Chapter 14.) It is essentially a neurological condition that often responds well to medication such as Ritalin. Remedial interventions such as help with reading difficulties and study problems can also be beneficial.

CONDUCT PROBLEMS

You may find yourself in psychotherapy for *conduct problems*: for example, stealing, running away from home, lying, setting fires, cutting school, vandalism, cruelty to animals or people, rape, picking fights, or using a weapon.

Psychotherapy is usually the treatment of choice, as these behaviors may be a way of trying to cope with an unpredictable and stressful environment, such as abuse at home or alcoholism. Sometimes these types of behaviors are a result of hyperactivity (see above discussion). When this is suspected, medication may be recommended.

EATING DISORDERS

Under this classification we include *anorexia nervosa*: eating extremely little (i.e., self-starvation), and *bulimia*: binge eating and vomiting. As much has been written on these disorders, we will not discuss them here in detail. For more information, consult the publications and agencies listed in the Appendix.

Easting disorders are usually treated with psychotherapy, and in some cases antidepressant medication. In extreme forms, particularly for anorexia nervosa, the person may need to be hospitalized.

OBSESSIVE-COMPULSIVE BEHAVIORS

People who are obsessive-compulsive are often perfectionists. They like order in their lives and want everything to be just right. They may go over and over something in their minds and talk continually about what is bothering them.

Obsessions

When you are obsessed, you can't stop thinking about something or someone. Perhaps it is a bad grade on a test, or a fight with a friend, or a person you have a crush on. An obsession becomes a problem when the thoughts keep coming to mind and you can't think of anything else. You may be afraid that something bad is going to happen to you, and you play the details over and over in your mind: What will happen? What might you do? Images come to your mind that you just can't shake.

Compulsions

You develop some actions to help you try to control the obsessive thoughts. These actions become *compulsive* in that you have to perform them over and over to make the thoughts and fears go away. Compulsive behaviors are an attempt to control aspects of your life that you may feel you cannot control. They may start out as childhood rituals or superstitions, such as always wearing the same clothes when you have an exam, or not stepping on cracks in the sidewalk, or washing your hands. But when they seem to take control of you instead of the other way around, you may have a serious problem.

Debbie

Debbie was afraid of germs. She would never drink out of another person's cup or taste others' ice cream cones. As she got older she found that she would wash her hands over and over, to the point that they were becoming very red and sore.

Now that Debbie was in high school she had to get up very early because it took her an hour to take a shower, to be clean enough. In college, when her friends would ask her to go out with them, she could never just go; she would have to take her shower first, and by then her friends were gone.

When Debbie got older and married, she couldn't leave the house each morning without scrubbing the kitchen floor thoroughly, getting down on her knees and into every corner. She had to get up at 5 in the morning to get everything done and was often late for work. Debbie never told anyone about this behavior, but it took up a huge part of her life. Her family thought she was just being fussy or slow. If she thought about skipping the ritual for a day, she felt herself getting very tense and anxious. The only thing that seemed to calm her down was to perform her ritualistic behaviors.

Through therapy and medication Debbie was able to calm her anxieties and to understand when this behavior had started and what caused it. Psychotherapy helped her to face her anxieties and gradually change her morning habits. She came to realize that nothing bad would happen if she stopped doing the tasks.

Medications and Treatments for Obsessive-Compulsive Disorders

Behavioral therapy can be helpful in learning to control the thoughts and behaviors associated with an obsessive compulsive disorder (OCD). Sometimes these behaviors seem to have a biological component and even to run in families. Other times they may have been caused by some bad experience, such as living in a family with an alcoholic or having been abused. When psychotherapeutic techniques do not seem to be working, you may consider medication.

Young children are usually not treated with medication for obsessive-compulsive behaviors. These repetitive behaviors may be a natural part of their growing up and learning to take control over their lives. However, teenagers and adults can often benefit from medication and psychotherapy. A medication frequently used is Anafranil (clomipramine), which can reduce the intensity of the symptoms although it does not usually make them go away entirely. More recently Prozac (fluoxetine), Zoloft (setraline), and Paxil (paroxetine) have been used successfully in treating persons with OCD. As mentioned earlier, some shakiness and lightheadedness may occur at first, until your body gets used to the medication and the dosage is properly adjusted for your system.

PSYCHOSIS

Psychotic behavior may include:

- irrational beliefs
- paranoia or extreme suspiciousness
- hallucinations (seeing things or hearing sounds that don't exist)

- withdrawing from people and staying alone
- clingy behavior (particularly toward parents)
- strange behavior
- extreme stubbornness
- rituals (doing something over and over again, such as hand-washing)
- deterioration of personal hygiene.

Any one of these behaviors alone does not necessarily mean a person is psychotic, but several of them together may indicate a serious mental disorder.

Medication and Treatment for Psychotic Behavior

Again a combination of psychotherapy and medication is used. The medication is referred to as *antipsychotic medication* or *major tranquilizers* and includes drugs such as Haldol (haloperidol), Stelazine (trifluoperazine), and Thorazine (chlorpromazine).

In recent years a new drug, Clozaril, has been used when the other drugs have not been effective.

These medications help the person feel more inner control and reduce the panic that comes from the irrational beliefs and hallucinations. Sometimes people who have severe mood swings also experience psychotic symptoms. They may be treated with Lithium and Tegretol (carbamazepine) to help these manic-depressive episodes.

The side effects of these medications may include extreme restlessness and involuntary movements of the face and body. In some cases the muscles may become tight or rigid.

You should notify your doctor if you experience any of these side effects. In most cases the symptoms are mild and disappear in a matter of days or weeks. In some cases, however, they can be serious. Your psychiatrist may need to adjust the medication, or you may need to try a different kind of medication that your body tolerates better.

PLEASE NOTE: In addition to the side effects discussed above, there are others that may be quite serious. They occur rarely, but you should not take any chances. If you don't feel well or notice any changes in your mood or body no matter how minor, tell your therapist, the psychiatrist, or the doctor who is giving you the medication. Keep your doctor informed, so she or he can make adjustments or changes. Don't try to guess and make changes yourself. And don't stop taking the medication without consulting the doctor. This is how people get into trouble with medication.

GETTING STARTED ON MEDICATION

Therapists who are not medical doctors (e.g., psychologists or social workers) refer patients to psychiatrists for medication. Psychiatrists are medically trained and in most states are the only mental health professionals who can legally prescribe medication. If your psychotherapist is a psychiatrist, there is no need for a referral. In areas where there is a shortage of psychiatrists, general-practice physicians prescribe the medication in consultation with your psychotherapist.

When your therapist suggests that you see a psychiatrist for medication, you may feel that he is trying to get rid of you, or that he cannot help you anymore. Or you may wonder, "Maybe he doesn't like me?" Actually, mental health professionals often work as a team. In referrals for medication you continue to see your therapist for your psychotherapy, and the psychiatrist follows you for the medication.

Visits to the psychiatrist for medication are less frequent than those for psychotherapy. The first visit will be rather long, perhaps an hour, as the therapist asks you many questions about yourself. She needs to understand your life-style, who lives with you, and how responsible you are. She may also want to get information about your medical condition or have a blood test or psychological testing.

A blood test may be needed periodically to monitor how the medication is building up in your system; this is sometimes referred to as getting the blood levels. The procedure is important so you won't get too much or too little for your system. The blood can be drawn in the doctor's office, or you may have to go to a lab.

After your initial visit, the following visits will most likely be shorter, fifteen to thirty minutes. You usually won't see the psychiatrist every week; future visits may be scheduled for every other week for a while, then once a month may be enough. At times you may be asked to contact the physician by phone, so you can tell her how you are feeling and if you are having any side effects.

STAY IN TOUCH WITH YOUR DOCTOR

If you take medication you need to keep in contact with your doctor, so it can be adjusted properly. *THIS IS VERY IMPORTANT.* Everyone's body is different, so you and your doctor need to see how the particular medication affects you. If you get any side effects, such as a headache or nervousness, tell your doctor so she can adjust the dosage. And if that particular medication doesn't seem to be working for you or if you get too many side effects, the doctor will take you off of it and find another drug that will be better for you. Just because one drug doesn't work doesn't mean that there aren't others that can help.

In recent years new medications have become available, and more and more are being developed and tested. Just because you or your parents know of someone who took medication and didn't seem to be helped, don't assume that that will be the case with you. Also, you may hear people say that someone took medication and got worse. Most of the time you don't really know the whole story. The friend may not have been taking his medication properly or keeping in contact with his doctor. Or he may have gotten worse for reasons unrelated to the medication. And who knows: He may have been even worse without the calming effects of the drugs.

STOPPING MEDICATION ON YOUR OWN

One of the more common problems is that people stop taking the medication too soon, because:

- they have been reluctant to take it in the first place and can't wait to stop it, or
- they begin to feel better and fail to realize that it is the medication that is making them feel better.

Once off the medication, their old symptoms return. In not too long they begin to feel bad again.

Going off and on the medication as you want to is not a good idea. Your body needs to adjust gradually to most of these drugs, and it may take a few weeks for you to feel the full effect and for your body to become adjusted to them. The same applies when you go off the medication.

If you stop abruptly, you may have severe withdrawal symptoms; you can make yourself very sick.

Talk with your doctor. He may have you gradually take less and less until you reach a level that is comfortable or until you are off the medication altogether. When you are under stress at a later time, you can talk with your doctor about possibly increasing the dosage again.

Kim

Kim became quite depressed at school. Eventually she was sent to see a therapist, but after weeks of therapy she was still not able to function. Her therapist suggested medication, but she refused. She knew that her parents would object. To them, taking medication for personal problems was a sign of weakness. It was not a part of their culture. Kim was afraid of medication and what it would do to her. She didn't like the idea of putting chemicals into her body. Also, by taking it, it would be telling her parents that she was really sick, mentally sick perhaps.

But as time went on, Kim was unable to do any of her schoolwork and was spending most of her time in her room. She no longer hung out with her friends and felt that they didn't like her anymore. When she told her therapist that she had been thinking of jumping out a window at school, the therapist became concerned. He told Kim that he was worried that she might actually kill herself. After talking with her for a while, they both agreed that she might feel safer and might get better quicker if she went to a hospital for a while.

In the hospital, to her surprise Kim felt a sense of relief. There were people around and people she could talk to. The pressures of school and her family were off for a while. She saw a therapist every day and began taking Zoloft, an antidepressant medication. After only a few days she began to feel better.

Her parents came to see her and met with the psychiatrist in charge. Although the hospitalization and medication were explained to them, they did not seem to understand what this was all about. They did not speak English well, and this was out of their cultural experience and customs.

When Kim went home from the hospital, her mother told her to stop taking the medication, that she could get better by herself if she just applied herself and studied harder. Kim stopped taking the medication. For a few days she felt fine. But gradually the sad thoughts began to return; her mind became cloudy again. She was easily distracted and couldn't concentrate on her work. She missed two appointments with her therapist. She was on a downward spiral again.

Fortunately the teachers at Kim's school began to notice that her school efforts were declining. She was encouraged to go back to her therapist and to go back on the medication. A translator was found to speak to her parents. Although they were still resistant to the idea of Western medicine, they had become alarmed at her behavior. They began to realize that her problems were not of her own making, that just trying harder didn't seem to be the solution. Kim continued in therapy and also on medication. She did not need to go to the hospital this time, as she got help before things got too bad. By the end of the school year she was almost back to her old self and was only on a very low dosage of medication.

WILL I BECOME ADDICTED?

You have heard about drug addiction; in fact, someone you know may be addicted to drugs. The mere idea of having to take medication scares you. You're afraid that you'll become addicted. You don't like the idea of being "dependent" upon something outside your body. You worry: "Maybe I'll get used to it." "Maybe I'll like it and not be able to stop." You wonder if you'll have to take medication all your life.

You should be aware that the antidepressants and the antipsychotics are not addicting. Some of the antianxiety drugs can be, but not all of them. (For example, the antianxiety drug Buspar is one that is not addictive.)

By "addictive" we are referring to abusing a drug, losing control, using it more and more until the drug has a bad effect on your body and your life. Should you develop a physical dependence, this would not mean that you could never get over it. You would need to withdraw from the drug under a physician's supervision, so that you tapered off slowly and properly. If not, you might get serious withdrawal or rebound symptoms.

On the other hand, you may be afraid that you will become psychologically dependent and like the feeling so much that you won't be able to stop taking the medication. For most people, however, the situation is the opposite; when they start feeling better, they stop taking the medication on their own. This can create severe physical problems, particularly if they stop suddenly rather than following the prescribed method of tapering off. Also, if they stop too soon, the unpleasant symptoms may come back again.

Some people do have "addictive personalities"; if you

feel you are one, you need to work closely with the physician prescribing the medication.

A *word of caution*: If you have or have had a drug or alcohol problem, be sure to discuss this with your doctor. If you are afraid that this new medication may get you hooked again or that you might take an overdose, tell the doctor. He or she can regulate the dosage and give you only a limited amount of pills at a time.

If anyone in your family has a drug or alcohol problem, be certain to keep your medication in a safe place, so that person can't get to it. Alcohol is essentially a drug and can be harmful if taken when you are also taking psychotropic medication. Just stopping your medication when you have an evening of partying so that you can drink doesn't help. Your medication builds up in your blood and is still there in high levels. Learn to drink club soda on ice, a Coke, or other soft drinks and still have a good time. You'll find that after a while you won't need the alcohol to feel good, once your medication is working. And you won't have to deal with hangovers.

MEDICATING YOURSELF

Sometimes when people feel bad about themselves or are depressed, they take a drink of alcohol or a street drug. If their bad feeling continues, they rely on alcohol or drugs as a way to feel better. But the feeling better that comes from this form of *self-medication* is short-lived and can be dangerous. And you can become addicted. The kind of drug-taking that we are talking about here is regulated by a doctor. You know the exact dosage that is in your system and you take not too much and not too little. You take only enough to help your negative symptoms but not to produce more problem behavior. You also know what is in

the drugs you get from the doctor. With street drugs you
are never sure how pure they are, how strong they are, or
what you are really taking.

AN IMPORTANT NOTE: Stay in touch with your doctor.
Do not medicate yourself.
The doctor has the training to
know what to do.

CHAPTER 14

Why Would They Want Me to Be Tested?

You're used to being tested all the time in school: classroom quizzes, big exams at midterm or the end of a semester, and those standardized achievement tests that they give every so often to an entire class.

"THE IDEA OF BEING TESTED MAKES ME NERVOUS."

Even though you've had to take tests of one kind or another almost all your life, the idea of taking a test probably still makes you a bit nervous. Most people no matter how old or how bright suffer some form of test anxiety. It's only natural. You want to perform well; you want others to think well of you; and maybe the results of the test will have some impact on your life.

Most tests that you take in school are given to you as part of a group. You haven't been singled out for the testing. But sometimes a teacher or counselor may suggest that you be tested alone, just you.

Worries, Worries . . . and Questions

The referral for *individual testing* may frighten you because you may not understand:

- why you have been chosen
- what kinds of questions they are going to ask you
- what the tests will tell them about you.

You may wonder what you have done, why you have been singled out. You may think that the test is some kind of punishment.

You worry that they will discover something about you that you will be ashamed of: "Perhaps I'm not as smart as people think I am. I'll be found out, caught as a fraud." "Maybe they'll find out that I'm crazy; after all, I heard them say that this was *psychological* testing."

You think testing is for mentally retarded people, and you remember everyone making jokes about "retards." You worry that your friends will tease you.

You wonder if somehow these tests can read your mind, and that they will discover some of your deep dark secrets.

"Maybe I won't do well. Maybe I won't be able to pass the tests," you may think to yourself.

Or you even worry about doing too well. Even now you find yourself lying to friends about your high scores or grades so they won't feel bad or avoid you. Although doing well on tests may open up doors for you, you worry that if you are too bright, the testing may set you apart from your friends, making you less popular or open to ridicule. Not cool. Acceptance and being part of the group are very important to teens.

WHY PSYCHOLOGICAL TESTING?

There are a variety of reasons why a person might be referred for psychological testing. Basically, referrals are made because more information is needed about your abilities and capabilities, or about your personality and behavior. The person initiating the referral may be a teacher, the school counselor, the school psychologist, or perhaps your parents or your psychotherapist. The person doing the testing is most often the school psychologist or a private psychologist outside the school system.

Sometimes a therapist or counselor feels it's important to gain a more in-depth understanding of your personality or abilities as soon as possible.

- Perhaps you have been acting in a strange or disruptive way and the therapist wants to know if you might have a serious mental disorder.
- Perhaps you are in therapy because of a court decision, and the court has requested the psychological testing to help make the best decisions about how to help you.
- Perhaps it is important to know how you might relate to certain stresses in your life.

The results of the testing may help answer questions, such as:

- Could you benefit from psychotherapy? Perhaps as a result of the testing, you may be referred for counseling or psychotherapy to help you with your problems.

- Are you in the best class for you? What kind of help might you need academically? Perhaps the school needs to make some decisions about you, such as placing you in a special class, giving you special help with your studies, or advising you about your abilities and future.

When the therapist has a better understanding of you, he or she can make more appropriate and more helpful suggestions.

Helen

Helen had been failing in her schoolwork this semester. She had been a very good student, but for some reason, she was no longer able to concentrate. When she sat down to study, her mind just wandered, not onto anything in particular, almost into a void. She found herself skipping her schoolwork, missing most of her classes, and just wandering the streets.

Helen never had many friends, but now she was avoiding the few she did have. When she was with them, she tried to put up a big front, acting really happy and bubbly. Perhaps that was why she tried to avoid them: The show just took more energy than she could muster. She had always prided herself on being an excellent student. Now she felt like she was nothing—a failure. Her family had always looked to her to be the successful one. Now she saw no future.

In desperation Helen wandered into the school counselor's office. She tried to describe how she felt, but everything was just so vague. The counselor met with her for several sessions but felt she didn't really understand the basis of Helen's problems, as they were presented in a very confused manner. The counselor suggested that Helen be tested by the school psychologist so they could try to determine what was going on.

At first Helen felt anxious. She wondered what they might find out in the testing that they did not already know. Would they find out all those strange thoughts that she was having? Would they tell her she was crazy? Her uncle had been very depressed at one time and was even sent to a hospital for a while. She didn't want that to happen to her.

However, with the counselor's encouragement, Helen agreed to take the tests. They were not as hard as she had thought; in fact, some of them were actually fun. But others were rather upsetting, as she couldn't figure out why they were showing her those pictures or asking her those questions.

Afterward, Helen was able to talk to the school psychologist about the results of her testing. The psychologist explained to her that the testing showed that she was suffering from what he called a "major depression." They talked about this diagnosis and what it meant to her. The psychologist explained that her lack of energy and difficulty concentrating on her work was related to depression. Helen had the ability to do her work but her emotional difficulties were getting in the way. The psychologist reassured her that depression was a condition that could be treated, and that she need not despair.

The school psychologist referred Helen to a therapist who worked with a clinic in her community.

The results of the testing were discussed with the new therapist with Helen's consent. The new therapist learned about Helen's depression and her low self-esteem. The testing helped Helen and her therapist identify her problems and gave more insight into what was bothering her in much less time than therapy alone could have done—particularly since Helen had such a difficult time expressing herself. In the end, Helen was able to progress more quickly in her treatment, as the therapist had a better understanding of her personality from the beginning.

"WHAT ARE THE TESTS LIKE?"

Let us look at some of the common reasons that students are referred for individual psychological testing. Then we'll discuss the kinds of tests that are usually given, and how the results are used. We'll also see what kinds of information the tests can provide about you and how this information can be used to help you. Referrals for individual psychological testing may include:

Personality tests to gain a better understanding of:

- your personal traits and emotional difficulties
- your psychological defenses or your typical ways of dealing with the world.

Intelligence and aptitude tests to gain a better understanding of:

- your abilities
- your academic potential.

Tests of special abilities to identify:

• possible learning disabilities
• special skills.

Interest inventories to help you make choices for your future

• by identifying your interests in work and leisure time.

Psychological tests are often given when there is a question about how someone is feeling or thinking. Sometimes a person's behavior suggests that something is wrong.

Terry

Terry may be acting out in class, being unruly, causing trouble. This is unlike him. The principal wonders why? Could Terry be depressed because his family has just moved into the school district. Are there other problems that the school doesn't know about? His parents don't seem to understand his behavior, and he refuses to discuss his problems with anyone. The testing won't give the exact answers about what is bothering him, but it can reveal if he is depressed or highly anxious, for example.

Joan

Joan was having trouble concentrating on her work and seemed to be falling behind in her studies. She was more quiet than usual and was not spending as much time with her friends. When she spoke to the school psychologist, she said that she just didn't have any energy and couldn't concentrate. When she did read, nothing made sense. Her memory too seemed not as good as it had been. Was Joan suffering from depression? Being sad can drain your energy and become so distracting that you can't study. Or was something else going on that interfered with her thinking? Perhaps through testing one could begin to understand better some of her problems and determine if there were psychological reasons underlying them.

Personality tests can be used to help you understand your emotional conflicts and by using this information to help you to deal with your life and the world. The results of the testing may help to:

- clarify some aspects of your behavior
- gain a better understanding of your emotional makeup
- identify your personal strengths and your typical ways of dealing with your problems
- identify problem areas that may not be readily evident
- confirm some ideas or hypotheses that the therapist has about how you are feeling or why you are acting the way you are.

Psychological Testing as a Help to Psychotherapy

Sometimes the results of psychological testing can be useful when one is in psychotherapy. In the case of Joan above, if Joan were to be referred to a therapist, the therapist could have a better understanding of some of Joan's problems. Of course you could say, "Well, why doesn't he just ask Joan?" But Joan may not really understand what is going on. In her case, she was very vague about her problems. All she knew was that she wasn't doing well in school and couldn't figure out why.

Personality testing can be helpful when the therapist is not sure about a diagnosis or a direction in which to go in your therapy. He may want or need more information about your emotional and cognitive makeup in a shorter period of time than the slow process of therapy would reveal. The testing is added information that the therapist can use to help the two of you in your work together. It helps the therapist to see how you perform under stress, how you solve problems, how you see yourself, and how you feel about yourself.

Personality tests do not always give direct answers, but they can provide insight into questions such as:

- Are you depressed? Might you try to kill yourself?
- Is your sexual behavior suggestive of antisocial tendencies?
- Are your fearfulness and shyness symptoms of some larger personality problem?
- Is your talking back to teachers or your parents a symptom of your feelings toward authority figures in general, or does it reflect your attitudes toward yourself and others?

Paper and Pencil Inventories

These personality inventories, as they are called, are often made up of a series of descriptive statements. You are asked to indicate which ones best describe you.

For example:

__ I feel sad most of the time.
__ I am anxious.
__ I jump when there is a loud bang.
__ People don't seem to like me.
__ I prefer to be by myself than with others.
__ I often have headaches.
__ I don't care what happens to me.
__ When I get bored, I usually stir up some excitement.

Interpreting results. The scores on a paper-and-pencil (or standardized) personality inventory gives you a place on a scale. The scores will show that you have checked items that describe you more in one direction than another. For example, your score may reveal that you are more of an extrovert (outgoing) than an introvert (reserved, shy); or that you tend to like to take charge rather than let others lead the way. Or your results may reveal that you are a team player rather than someone who prefers to work on your own. Or the opposite could be so.

Some inventories compare you to a large group of others who have answered the same questions. The widely used MMPI (Minnesota Multiphasic Personality Inventory) gives scores that describe your emotional makeup: for example, to what extent you are depressed, manic (hyperactive), or paranoid (overly suspicious). The MMPI was originally normed (or tested) on people with serious mental illnesses, and it is not always easy to make sense of the scores when used with others, particularly young people.

Teenagers are often testing the limits of social interaction and learning about themselves. It is a very trying time. Teens tend to be introspective, and their questioning of life and their frustrations in growing up may show as mental illness on a test when in fact they are within the appropriate range of emotions for their age. Thus, it is very important that you take personality inventories only when you know that they will be interpreted by a highly qualified and experienced person, someone who has had a lot of experience testing young people.

Projective Tests

In this group of tests are those that have little structure and allow you to express yourself and "project" your feelings onto what you see. In the course of doing this, you also reveal how you feel about yourself and how you see the world and others in it. These are not standardized tests like the paper and pencil inventories; that is, your responses are not compared directly to other people's scores to see where you stand. To interpret projective tests, the psychologists must rely on their clinical judgment, which comes from years of training and experience. Thus, only clinical psychologists with their special training in testing are allowed to administer projective tests in most states.

The Rorschach Ink Blot Technique

One of the most famous projective tests is the Rorschach Ink Blot Technique. In this test you are shown a series of large ink blots—some made from black ink on a white background, and others from colored ink. You are asked to use your imagination to describe what you see. Since these are formless blots of ink, you bring your own experiences and ideas to the test; you are free to see what you want to see.

There are, however, "popular" responses, that is, those that most people do give. But that does not mean that these are "right" responses. People who are creative might give a lot of unique responses. On the other hand, people with serious mental illnesses may give very bizarre responses. Psychologists with their training understand the differences among these many types of responses. The psychologist looks for the way you see the inkblot. Do you use details or the whole blot? Are you original? Is what you see something that makes sense, even if it isn't popular. Or is it strange or bizarre?

Thematic Apperception Test (TAT)

The TAT consists of a series of black-and-white pictures printed on large cards. Most of the pictures show people in some setting. You are asked to tell a story and to describe who you think the people are, what they are doing, and how they are feeling.

Again the interpretation is made in conjunction with other information about you. But your stories can give some indication about how you see the world and how you see yourself fitting into that world. Your responses can also give indications of aspects of your relationships with others, including areas of conflict.

For example, if you see angry men in most of the pictures, it may reveal how you feel about some of the men in your life, perhaps your father, stepfather, brother. If you see someone performing a noble act, such as rescuing another person, the story may suggest that you like to think of yourself as a good helpful person; or perhaps you are the one who wants to be rescued.

Draw-a-Person Test

You may be asked to draw a picture of yourself, or your family, or just a man or a woman. Sometimes you will be asked to draw a house, or a tree, as well. With younger children, these drawings can be revealing about developmental level, as at certain ages children tend to add more details and have more control over what they are drawing than at earlier ages. These drawings can also be useful in revealing how you see yourself in respect to others. The psychologist doesn't look to see what a great artist you are. He uses this as just one more piece of information about your self-concept and view of the world.

Bender-Gestalt

This test consists of a series of black-and-white designs (circles, squares, lines, etc.). You are asked to copy the designs onto a piece of paper. Again this is not a test of how well you can draw, but more a test of your ability to perceive, conceptualize, and organize what you see. It may reveal how your mind processes material that does not require reading; Can you see something, take it into your brain for processing, and then have it come back out through your being able to draw it (called eye-hand coordination). People with perceptual problems related to neurological problems, eye problems, brain injury, or learning disabilities may have difficulty with these drawings. Emotional problems can also affect the way people perceive and draw the designs. On the other hand, many people find this test quite fun, and try to see how well they can reproduce what they have seen.

In summary: Projection tests

The projective tests are highly controversial, as they do rely to a large part on the subjective judgment of the clinician. But they are useful, particularly when making decisions about whether or not someone is psychotic, that is, whether or not the person is out of touch with reality. They are also useful for understanding a person's inner conflicts, their defenses (e.g., the way they usually react to stress), depression, creativity, and rigidity and conformity. But projective tests should never be used alone. They should always be used in conjunction with other tests, clinical interviews, and other information about the person.

Some people are afraid that they will reveal something about themselves in these projective tests that they don't want others to know. Perhaps you have been very depressed and feeling suicidal. You are not sure what the psychologist will do if she finds that out. However, if you reveal emotional problems on these tests, the psychologist has the resources to work with you to overcome your difficulties.

TESTS OF MENTAL ABILITIES

Group Testing

In this category we have the paper-and-pencil tests of intelligence, aptitude, and achievement that are administered to everyone in a class together.

Intelligence tests tend to give a global score of your overall reasoning ability. Psychologists may look at how you perform on certain sub-tests as compared to others and how you approach the different tasks to make clinical judgments that go beyond the actual objective scores.

Aptitude tests are more specific in what they show in terms of your specific mental abilities. These tests give indications of your individual strengths and weaknesses, as well as indications of how you are doing in comparison to others in areas such as:

- verbal skills: reading, spelling, comprehension
- numerical skills: arithmetic computation, arithmetic reasoning (reading problems)
- spatial reasoning: solving problems that do not rely on numbers or words
- clerical aptitude: ability to do detail work that relies on eye-hand coordination and speed (such as copying designs, words, or numbers very quickly).

Achievement tests measure your knowledge in subjects that are related to what you learn in school: social studies, math, history, and so forth.

Individual Testing

Tests given to you on a one-to-one basis can offer more insight into your abilities than those given to you in a group setting. Many of the skill areas are the same as those tapped by group tests; however, because you are tested alone on these individual tests, it is possible to spend more time with you, covering more areas and going into greater depth. Also the examiner has the opportunity to see how you in particular solve problems and handle different tasks: some timed, some not, some requiring reading, others not.

Important areas in which you can demonstrate your skills are:

- problem-solving
- concentration
- short-term and long-term memory
- eye-hand coordination
- general information
- ability to think logically
- ability to form concepts based on verbal or written material
- ability to form concepts with nonverbal material, such as designs or numbers

Although teachers gain an understanding of students just by knowing them in the classroom, sometimes they are not sure just how hard to push a student:

- Is the student really working up to his or her capacity?
- Are there other ways of helping the student to learn by using the student's special strengths?

Test results can help teachers know what you are capable of, and thus they can gear their teaching toward the ways in which you learn best. Also, if there are any special services available, such as help with reading, writing, or math, you can take advantage of these. Or if you are gifted in certain areas, special programs may be available for you.

Intelligence Tests

The most popular individual intelligence tests are the Wechsler Scales: The Wechsler Intelligence Tests for

Adults–Revised (WAIS-R), and the Wechsler Intelligence Tests of Children-Revised (WISC-R). These tests are made up of about ten sub-tests or scales, each quite different from the other. Another individual intelligence test that is often used is the Stanford-Binet.

The so-called tests of intelligence were originally developed to identify those who are severely mentally retarded or those who are extremely gifted. The idea was that special classes would be set up to help maximize their learning. However, over the years the tests have been used (and sometimes misused) to place students in classes according to their level of understanding or to try to determine if students were working up to their abilities. They are also used as diagnostic tools to gain more insight into what a student knows and how he or she solves problems.

Although I cannot give you examples of exact questions, I can give you an idea of what some of the tests may be like. For example, you may be asked questions, such as:

"In what direction would you travel if you were flying from New York to California?" (Answer: West).

"In what way are a cat and a dog alike?" (Answer: Both are animals, or both have four legs).

You may be given:

• puzzles to put together
• a set of pictures to put in order to tell a story
• pictures or objects to identify
• arithmetic problems
• a short list of words, letters, or numbers to memorize and repeat back.

Interpreting the Results.   How you do on all these tests is then used as an estimate of your overall learning ability or intellectual functioning. The Wechsler tests have been given to thousands and thousands of people of all ages; thus, your performance can be compared to the performance of others the same age as you. Where do you stand: Is your overall intellectual functioning in the average range, in the above-average range, or in the below-average range.

The actual score is of less value than your relative standing to others. When compared to your performance in school and your school grades, the tests may suggest that you have abilities that for some reason you are not using. When interpreted along with the personality tests the results may suggest that you are having some conflicts in your life, perhaps with your family, that are making it hard for you to concentrate and thus affecting how well you do in school. The tests are only guides and indicators of what your capabilities are.

You may be afraid that these tests will show that you aren't as smart as you'd like people to think you are. Usually the tests reveal no big surprises, but in some cases the results may suggest that a person is in a class that is too difficult for her current level of functioning, or that she could use some special help with certain skills, like reading, arithmetic, or study skills. When used for the purposes for which they were designed, the tests of intelligence, aptitude, and achievement can be tools that help you become the person you would like to be.

Caution.   The major misuse of these tests is that uninformed people may look at an individual score and think that it tells all there is to know about the person. They may think that this represents how smart a person is and that the person won't be able to change. They may label a person without taking into consideration the many factors that go into performance at a given day and time. If someone has had a more intellectually stimulating home environment or better early school training, this will be reflected in the scores. Although some people may be naturally smarter than others, even the scores on so-called intelligence tests are affected by what you've been exposed to in your life.

The scores are, however, fairly good predictors of how well someone is expected to perform in school. But what goes into a person's test performance (as well as school performance) is a mixture of "nature and nurture," that is, what you are born with and what you experience in life.

Some people mistakenly think that someone who scores only a few points higher than another person is superior. But the test scores, although relatively stable, can vary by a few points if the test is repeated, so small differences between scores are essentially meaningless in practical terms.

These are only a few of the complex reasons why it is important that a qualified person administer and interpret the test results. Usually that person is a state-certified psychologist who understands the limits of the scores and is able to make appropriate inferences from them. Your performance on these tests of mental abilities must be considered as only a part of the total picture that is you.

TESTING IN SPECIAL AREAS: LEARNING DISABILITIES

If you seem to be doing okay in most areas but are having problems in specific areas such as reading, writing, spelling, or math, you may have what is commonly referred to as a specific *learning disability* (LD). This is a catch-all term that refers to a set of deficits or weaknesses that may have a neurological basis. This is an area that is not well understood, but I tend to think of LD as a "misfiring" of some nerve connections. Given the complexity of our brains, it would not be surprising that in some cases not everything is working one hundred percent, thus making it difficult to do all tasks equally well.

You may have heard of dyslexia, a learning disability in the area of reading and verbal skills. In Chapter 13 we discussed attention deficit disorder (ADD), a learning disability in which people have difficulty focusing their attention on their work. They become easily distracted, which affects their reading and study skills and results in academic difficulties. Specific learning disabilities may also show up in areas such as math.

Learning disabilities can be identified through testing. The clinician looks for a pattern of strengths and weaknesses in different areas to see where the problems lie. Then strategies can be devised that help you manage these problems and use your own strengths to your advantage.

Joe

Joe was basically a bright fellow who could talk and think his way through most things. But reading was a real struggle. He was a very slow reader and had trouble spelling. Often he reversed letters in words (and he found himself reversing numbers in math problems too). The slow reading made it difficult for him to keep up with his work. In elementary school he did well, but in high school where there was much more reading and the work became more difficult, he found himself falling further and further behind.

He felt ashamed and tried to cover up for his frustrations by being the class clown. He was always causing disturbances and even began cutting classes. That, of course, didn't help him in school.

Eventually the school psychologist had a conference with Joe's parents. Since he had been a good student and presented himself as generally bright, they suspected a "learning disability." Testing revealed that Joe indeed did reverse letters and numbers and that he had difficulty understanding what he read. His concentration was poor, and at times he had trouble putting his thoughts into logical order. And as Joe already knew, his reading speed was quite slow.

Joe had been afraid that he would be labeled "retarded." He wasn't so sure he was happy with the label "learning disabled" or, as the psychologist said, "dyslexic." Dyslexia refers to a specific learning disability that involves verbal skills, such as slow reading, the reversal of letters when reading or spelling, and difficulty understanding or remembering what you have read.

Joe's testing turned out to be helpful. For once it was discovered that he had problems, Joe was able to get help to learn how to work around them. He learned to speed-read and also learned how to organize his work. His teachers were informed of his specific difficulties, and as a result they allowed him to have extra time on tests and assignments when needed.

At first Joe felt funny being singled out like this. But as time went on and as his work improved, he began to feel better about himself. He knew that he could do the work; he knew he wasn't "stupid." Now he was able to show everyone. Joe also was encouraged to get tape recordings of books from the library, when he found that reading printed books took too long and was too difficult. He was surprised to learn how many books were available on tape. Sometimes he would listen to the tape and then also read the book. The tape made the reading so much easier.

Learning disabilities are not well understood, and there isn't really a test that can say, "Yes, here it is, this is dyslexia or some other specific learning disability." But those with experience in this area can use the test results in conjunction with what they know about the person's performance in school to make such a clinical diagnosis. Once made, appropriate help can then be made available.

INTEREST INVENTORIES AND VOCATIONAL APTITUDE TESTS

Among the assessment instruments available to you are those that help you to identify your areas of interest and your career possibilities. These inventories or tests are constructed in such a way that you must make choices between things that you might like to do:

- Would you rather be an artist or work in business?
- Would you rather work outdoors or indoors?
- Would you prefer to take care of someone who is sick or work in an office?
- Would you prefer to be an artist or take care of someone who is sick?

The way you make your choices on these inventories reflects your preferences and results in a pattern of interests: what you'd like to do and what you'd not like to do. On some inventories, like the Strong Interest Inventory, your responses are compared to the responses of people who are working in different fields, to see in which work areas your interests lie.

Interests are only part of the picture, however, as you need to look at your abilities as well. Taking both into consideration, your therapist or counselor can then use the results to stimulate discussion about your future, and help you to make decisions about how to prepare for what you'd like to do.

ASK FOR A FOLLOW-UP REPORT

Don't be afraid to ask the psychologist for a follow-up on how you performed on the testing. Tell her that you want to know what your strengths and weaknesses are, and what she can tell you about yourself. Tell her you would like to know these things so that you can better understand yourself and make good choices as you go through life.

The psychologist probably won't give your exact scores, for as I mentioned these are often misunderstood and thus misused by people. But she should be able to tell you:

- how well you performed in general for your class or age group: Were you in the average range, above average, or below average?
- where you did particularly well?
- what areas need to be developed; are you working up to your potential?
- how you handle stressful situations, and

- how you feel about yourself and your relationships with others.

If you have an individual psychotherapist, he or she could get a report from the test administrator with your permission, and could interpret the results for you in light of what has been going on in the psychotherapy.

THE TESTING IS FOR YOU

Do your best whenever you are tested, and do not worry so much about how well you will do. Everyone has their strengths and weaknesses. Since you can't study for most psychological tests, it is best to take them with a clear head. Be sure to get enough sleep the night before. Arrive a bit early to the testing, if possible, so you will be relaxed.

Remind yourself: "The testing is for my benefit. I will do the best I can and that's all I can do."

CHAPTER ◇ 15

Overview: A Course in Yourself

Most people don't read straight through a book such as this one; they pick and choose chapters or sections that are of particular interest to them. Let us review here some of the chapters to help you organize what you have read and to suggest other chapters you might wish to read.

Identifying Your Problems

The first four chapters are designed to help you to decide if you could benefit from talking to someone about your problems, and if this someone should be a mental health professional.

Making a Good Choice

Chapters 5 to 10 explain what goes on in therapy and counseling. There are suggestions about kinds of questions to ask and what to expect during the first session. You are also given specific steps to take to find a therapist and to make sure that the therapist is qualified and is the right person for you.

Finding Answers for Your Special Concerns

Chapters 11 to 14 are about specific situations that may be of concern to you: paying for therapy, confidentiality, taking medication, taking psychological tests.

Locating Other Sources of Information

At the end of the book is an Appendix called *Resources*, which lists national agencies or organizations that are prepared to help you find a therapist, a support group, or mental health clinic. They also provide printed material, such as small brochures, that give you information about the problems you may be concerned with, for example, eating disorders, physical or sexual abuse, drug or alcohol abuse, depression or anxiety. There is also a section called For Further Reading, listing books and other publications. These may be available in your local public library or school library.

After reading this book and some of the resource material, you may decide that going into therapy is just what you need to do. *Just remember*: Psychotherapy is like taking a course in school, except in this case the subject you are trying to understand is . . . YOU.

Appendix: Resources

Following is a list of organizations at which you can speak with someone, find out about support groups, and get brochures or other informational publications. You may also find local chapters of these organizations listed in your telephone directory. Those marked with a (T) can direct you to therapists in your community. Your school's counselor, student health service, or community mental health center are other sources of information regarding local support groups and therapists.

ABUSE: ALCOHOL AND DRUG

Alcoholics Anonymous
P.O. Box 459, Grand Central Station
New York, NY 10163
1-800-637-6237
(212) 686-1100

Alateen and Al-Anon
Al-Anon Family Group Headquarters
P.O. Box 862, Midtown Station
New York, NY 10018-0862
1-800-344-2666
(212) 302-7240

Cocaine Anonymous
3740 Overland Avenue
Los Angeles, CA 90034

800-COCAINE
P.O. Box 100
Summit, NJ 07901
1-800-COCAINE
1-800-262-2463

Children of Alcoholics Foundation
540 Madison Avenue
New York, NY 10022
(212) 980-5394

Narcotics Anonymous
World Service Office
P.O. Box 9999
Van Nuys, CA 91409

National Institute on Drug Abuse
5600 Fishers Lane
Rockville, MD 20857
(1-800-662-HELP)
(301) 443-6480

National Institute on Alcohol Abuse and Alcoholism
5600 Fishers Lane
Rockville, MD 20857
(301) 443-3885

Alcohol and Drug Abuse Problems Association of
    America, Inc.
444 North Capitol Street NW
Washington, DC 20001
(202) 737-4340

Alcohol, Drug Abuse, and Mental Health Administration
5600 Fishers Lane
Rockville, MD 20857
(301) 443-3783

National Clearinghouse for Alcohol and Drug Information
P.O. Box 2345
Rockville, MD 20852
(301) 468-2600

National Council on Alcoholism and Drug Dependence,
    Inc.
12 West 21st Street
New York, NY 10010
1-800-NCA-CALL
(212) 206-6770

National Drug Abuse Information and Treatment Referral
    Hotline
National Institute on Drug Abuse
12280 Wilkins Avenue
Rockville, MD 20852
1-800-662-HELP
1-800-66-AYUDA   (for Spanish-speaking callers)

National Federation of Parents for Drug-Free Youth
8730 Georgia Avenue
Silver Spring, MD 20910
1-800 554-KIDS

ABUSE: PHYSICAL AND SEXUAL

American Association for Protecting Children
The American Humane Association
63 Inverness Drive East
Englewood, CO 80112
(303) 792-9900

C. Henry Kempe National Center for the Prevention and
Treatment of Child Abuse and Neglect
Department of Pediatrics—UCHSC
1205 Oneida Street
Denver, CO 81220
(303) 321-3963

Childhelp USA
National Headquarters
6463 Independence Avenue
Woodland Hills, CA 91367

or

Childhelp USA
East Coast Regional Office
913 King Street
Alexandria, VA 22314
(703) 739-5893

National Child Abuse Hot Line of Childhelp USA:
1-800-4-A-CHILD
1-800-422-4453

National Committee for Prevention of Child Abuse
332 South Michigan Avenue
Chicago, IL 60604
(312) 663-3520

National Domestic Violence Hotline
P.O. Box 7032
Huntington Woods, MI 48070
1-800-SAFE
1-800-6363   (for hearing impaired)

VOICES in Action
    (Victims of Incest Can Emerge Survivors in Action)
P.O. Box 148309
Chicago, IL
(312) 327-1500

RUNAWAYS

National Runaway Hotline: 1-800-231-6946

AIDS AND OTHER SEXUALLY TRANSMITTED DISEASES

Centers for Disease Control Hotline:　　1-800-342-AIDS

Spanish-Language　1-800-344-SIDA
Hearing Impaired　1-800-243-7889　　TDD/TTY

ANXIETY, PHOBIAS, OBSESSIVE-COMPULSIVE DISORDER

Anxiety Disorders Association of America (T)
6000 Executive Boulevard
Rockville, MD 20852-3801
(301) 231-9350

National Center for the Treatment of Phobias, Anxiety
　and Depression
1755 S Street NW
Washington, DC 20009
(202) 363-7792

Obsessive-Compulsive Disorder Foundation, Inc. (T)
P.O. Box 9573
New Haven CT 06535
(203) 772-0565

Women Helping Agoraphobics, Inc.
P.O. Box 4900
South Framingham, MA 01701

AUTISM

Autism Society of America
1234 Massachusetts Avenue NW
Washington, DC 20005

DEPRESSION AND MANIC-DEPRESSION

Depressives Anonymous
329 East 62nd Street
New York NY 10021
(212) 689-2600

Lithium Information Center
c/o Department of Psychiatry
University of Wisconsin
600 Highland Avenue
Madison, WI 53792
(608) 263-6171

National Depressive and Manic-Depressive Association
53 West Jackson Boulevard
Chicago, IL 60604
(312) 939-2442

National Foundation for Depressive Illness
P.O. Box 2257
New York, NY 10116
(212) 268-4260

SUICIDE

American Association of Suicidology
2459 South Ash Street
Denver, CO 80222
(303) 692-0985

The Compassionate Friends   (for family & friends)
900 Jorie Boulevard
Oak Bridge, IL 60522
(312) 323-5010

National Committee of Youth Suicide Prevention
666 Fifth Avenue
New York NY 10103
(212) 957-9292

EATING DISORDERS

American Anorexia/Bulimia Association Inc.
133 Cedar Lane
Teaneck, NJ 07666
(201) 836-1800

National Associations of Anorexia Nervosa and Associated
    Disorders   (T)
Box 7
Highland, Park, IL 60035
(312) 831-3438

National Anorexic Aid Society   (T)
5796 Karl Road
Columbus, OH 43229
(614) 436-1112
(614) 846-2833

Overeaters Anonymous
Box 92870
Los Angeles, CA 90009
(213) 542-8363

Overeaters Anonymous
4025 Spencer Street
Torrance, CA 90503
(310) 618-8835

HYPERACTIVITY, ATTENTION DEFICIT DISORDERS, LEARNING DISABILITIES

Association for Children and Adults with Learning
 Disabilities
4156 Library Road
Pittsburgh, PA 15227
(412) 881-2253

Children with Attention Deficit Disorders (CHADD Inc.)
1859 North Pine Island Road
Plantation, FL 33322
(305) 587-3700

PARENT-CHILD CONFLICTS

Families Anonymous World Service Office
P.O. Box 528
Van Nuys, CA 91408
(818) 989-7841
1-800-736-9805

POSTTRAUMATIC STRESS

Anxiety Disorders Association of America
6000 Executive Boulevard
Rockville, MD 20852
(301) 231-9350

OTHER MENTAL HEALTH AGENCIES AND ORGANIZATIONS

American Academy of Child and Adolescent Psychiatry
3615 Wisconsin Avenue, NW
Washington, DC 20016
(202) 966-7300

American Academy of Pediatrics
PO Box 927
Elk Grove Village, ILL 60007
(312) 228-5005

American Association of Psychiatric Services for Children
2075 Scottsville Road
Rochester, NY 14623
(716) 436-4442

American College Health Association
1300 Piccard Drive
Rockville MD 20850
(301) 963-1100

American Family Therapy Association   (T)
2020 Pennsylvania Avenue NW
Washington DC 20006
(202) 994-2776

American Pediatrics Society
450 Clarkson Avenue
Brooklyn, NY 11203
(718) 270-1692

American Psychiatric Association   (T)
1400 K Street NW
Washington DC 20005
(202) 682-6000

American Psychological Association   (T)
750 First Avenue NE
Washington, DC 20002-4242
(202) 336-5500

American Society for Adolescent Psychiatry
24 Green Valley Road
Wallingford, PA 19086
(215) 566-1054

Association for the Advancement of Behavioral Therapy (T)
15 West 36th Street
New York, NY 10018
(212) 279-7970

Association for the Care of Children's Health
3615 Wisconsin Avenue, NW
Washington DC 20016
(202) 244-1801

Center for Cognitive Therapy   (T)
University of Pennsylvania
133 South 36th Street
Philadelphia, PA 19104
(215) 898-4100

Child Welfare League of America, Inc.
440 First Street NW
Washington, DC 20001
(202) 638-2952

Emotions Anonymous—Children (ages 5–13)
   (Self-help group)
Emotions Anonymous—Youth (ages 13–19)
P.O. Box 4245
St. Paul, MN 55104
(612) 647-9712

National Association for the Advancement of
   Psychoanalysis and the American Board for
   Accreditation and Certification, Inc. (T)
80 Eighth Avenue
New York, NY 10011
(212) 741-0515

National Alliance for the Mentally Ill
2101 Wilson Boulevard
Arlington, VA 22201
(703) 524-7600
(800) 950-NAMI   (for support group)

National Alliance for Research on Schizophrenia and
    Depression
208 South LaSalle Street
Chicago, IL 60604
(312) 641-1666

National Association of Social Workers   (T)
7981 Eastern Avenue
Silver Spring, MD 20910
(202) 408-8600

National Council of Community Mental Health Centers
12300 Twinbrook Parkway
Rockville MD 20852
(301) 984-6200

National Mental Health Consumer Self-Help
    Clearinghouse
311 South Juniper Street
Philadelphia, PA 19107
(215) 735-6367

National Institute of Mental Health
Public Inquiries Branch
5600 Fishers Lane
Rockville, MD 20857
(301) 443-4513

National Mental Health Association
1021 Prince Street
Alexandria, VA 22314
(703) 684-7722

For Further Reading

MENTAL HEALTH AND PSYCHOTHERAPY

Buckalew, M.W. *Learning to Control Stress*, rev.ed. New York: Rosen Publishing Group, 1982.

Carter, Sharon. *Coping through Friendship*. New York: Rosen Publishing Group, 1988.

Engler, John, and Goleman, Daniel. *The Consumer's Guide to Psychotherapy*. New York: Simon & Schuster/Fireside, 1992.

Gelinas, Paul J. *Coping with Anger*, rev.ed. New York: Rosen Publishing Group, 1988.

Simpson, Caroline, and Simpson, Dwain, rev.ed. *Coping with Emotional Disorders*. New York: Rosen, 1991.

Grosshandler, Janet. *Coping with Verbal Abuse*. New York: Rosen Publishing Group, 1989.

AIDS

Hein, K., and Foy, T. *AIDS: Trading Fears for Facts: A Guide for Young People*. New York: Consumers Union, 1991.

Kurland, M.L. *Coping with AIDS: Facts and Fears*, rev.ed. New York: Rosen Publishing Group, 1990.

ANXIETY, PHOBIAS, OBSESSIVE-COMPULSIVE DISORDERS

Greist, J.H., Jefferson, J.W., and Marks, I.M. *Anxiety and Its Treatment: Help Is Available.* Washington, DC: American Psychiatric Press, 1986.

Insel, T.R. ed. *New Findings in Obsessive-Compulsive Disorder.* Washington, DC: American Psychiatric Press, Inc., 1984.

Sheehan, D.V. *The Anxiety Disease and How to Overcome It.* New York: Charles Scribner's Sons, 1984.

Taylor, C.B., and Amow, B. *The Nature and Treatment of Anxiety Disorders.* New York: Free Press, 1988.

Webb, Margot. *Coping with Compulsive Behavior.* New York: Rosen Publishing Group, 1993.

CHILDHOOD DISORDERS

Looney, J.G., ed. *Chronic Mental Illness in Children and Adolescents.* Washington, DC: American Psychiatric Press, Inc., 1988.

Love, H.D. *Behavior Disorders in Children: A Book for Parents.* Springfield, IL: Thomas, 1987.

Wender, P.H. *The Hyperactive Child, Adolescent, and Adult: Attention Deficit Disorder Through the Lifespan.* New York: Oxford University Press, 1987.

Wing, L. *Autistic Children: A Guide for Parents and Professionals.* New York: Brunner/Mazel, 1985.

DEATH

Buckingham, Robert, and Huggard, Sandra. *Coping with Grief.* New York: Rosen Publishing Group, 1991.

Grosshandler, Janet. *Coping When a Parent Dies.* New York: Rosen Publishing Group, 1993.

Raab, Robert A. *Coping with Death,* rev.ed. New York: Rosen Publishing Group, 1989.

DEPRESSION AND MANIC-DEPRESSION

Bohn, J.R., and Jefferson J.W. *Lithium and Manic Depression: A Guide.* Madison, WI: University of Wisconsin, 1990.

Clayton, Lawrence, and Carter, Sharon. *Coping with Depression.* New York: Rosen Publishing Group, 1993.

DePaulo, J.R., and Ablo, D. *How to Cope with Depression: A Complete Guide for You and Your Family.* Cliffside, NJ: McGraw Hill, 1989.

Greist, J., and Jefferson, J.W. *Depression and Its Treatment: Help for the Nation's #1 Mental Problem.* Washington, DC: American Psychiatric Press, Inc., 1986.

Ottens, Allen J. *Coping with Romantic Breakup.* New York: Rosen Publishing Group, 1985.

Papolos, D., and Papolos, J. *Overcoming Depression.* New York: Harper & Row, 1987.

DIVORCE

Krementz, J. *How It Feels When Parents Divorce* (ages 8–16). New York: Knopf, 1988.

Raab, Robert A. *Coping with Divorce* rev.ed. New York: Rosen Publishing Group, 1984.

DRUG AND ALCOHOL ABUSE

Ball, Jacqueline. *Everything You Need to Know about Drug Abuse*, rev.ed. New York: Rosen Publishing Group, 1992.

Bartimole, C., and Bartimole, J. *Teenage Alcoholism and Substance Abuse.* Hollywood, FL: Compact Books, 1986.

Black, K.C. *It Will Never Happen To Me (Children of Alcoholics as Youngsters, Adolescents, and Adults).* New York: Ballantine, 1981.

Chatlos, C. *Crack.* New York: Putman, 1987.

Cohen, S., and Cohen, D. *A Six-Pack and a Fake ID: Teens Look at the Drinking Question.* New York: Dell, 1986.

Daley, D.C. *Surviving Addictions*. New York: Gardiner Press, 1987.

Grosshandler, Janet. *Coping with Alcohol Abuse*. New York: Rosen Publishing Group, 1990.

Inhalants. U.S. Department of Health and Human Services, National Institute on Drug Abuse Publication No. 83-1307. Washington, DC: Superintendent of Documents, U.S. Government Printing Office, 1983.

Ketcham, K., and Mueller, A. *Recover*. New York: Bantam Books, 1987.

McFarland, Rhoda. *Coping with Substance Abuse*, rev.ed. New York: Rosen Publishing Group, 1990.

Myers, J. *Staying Sober*. New York: Congdon & Weed, 1987.

Opiates. U.S. Department of Health and Human Services, National Institute on Drug Abuse Publication No. 84-1308. Washington, DC: Superintendent of Documents, U.S. Government Printing Office, 1984.

Ryan, E.A. *Straight Talk about Drugs and Alcohol*. New York: Dell, 1989.

When Cocaine Affects Someone You Love. U.S. Department of Health and Human Services, National Institute on Drug Abuse Publication No. 88-1559. Washington, DC: Superintendent of Documents, U.S. Government Printing Office, 1987.

EATING DISORDERS

Boone C., and O'Neil, N. *Starving for Attention: A Young Woman's Struggle and Triumph Over Anorexia Nervosa*. Minneapolis, MN: CompCare Pub, 1992.

Hall, L., and Cohn, L. *Bulimia: A Guide to Recovery*. Carlsbad, CA: Gurze Books, 1992.

Hirschmann, J.R., and Munter, C.H. *Overcoming Overeating*. New York: Fawcett Combine, Ballantine Books, 1988.

Elizabeth, L. *Twelve Steps for Overeaters*. New York: Hazelton Books/Harper Collins Pub., 1988.

Levenkron, S. *The Best Little Girl In the World*, rev.ed. New York: Warner, 1981.

Miller, P. *If I'm So Smart Why Do I Eat Like This?* New York: Warner, 1988.

Miller, P.M. *The Hilton Head Diet for Children and Teenagers.* New York: Warner Books, 1992.

Moe, Barbara. *Coping with Eating Disorders.* New York: Rosen Publishing Group, 1991.

Roth, G. *Why Weight: A Guide to End Compulsive Overeating.* New York: Penguin (Plume), 1989.

Saker, I.M., and Zimmer, M.A. *Dying to Be Thin: Understanding and Defeating Anorexia Nervosa and Bulimia—A Practical, Lifesaving Guide.* New York: Warner, 1987.

LEARNING DISABILITIES AND ACADEMIC PROBLEMS

Clayton, Lawrence, and Morrison, Jaydene. *Coping with a Learning Disability.* New York: Rosen Publishing Group, 1992.

Ottens, Allen J. *Coping with Academic Anxiety*, rev.ed. New York: Rosen Publishing Group, 1991.

PARENTS AND FAMILIES

Blomquist, Geraldine M., and Blomquist, Paul. *Coping as a Foster Child.* New York: Rosen Publishing Group, 1991.

Clayton, Lawrence. *Coping with a Drug Abusing Parent.* New York: Rosen Publishing Group, 1991.

Cohen, Shari. *Coping with Being Adopted.* New York: Rosen Publishing Group, 1988.

Jamiolkowski, Raymond. *Coping in a Dysfunctional Family.* New York: Rosen Publishing Group, 1993.

Kaplan, Leslie S. *Coping with Stepfamilies.* New York: Rosen Publishing Group, 1991.

Kurland, Morton L. *Coping with Family Violence*. New York: Rosen Publishing Group, 1990.

Miller, Deborah. *Coping When a Parent Is Gay*. New York: Rosen Publishing Group, 1992.

Potterfield, Kay, and Marie. *Coping with an Alcoholic Parent*, rev.ed. New York: Rosen Publishing Group, 1990.

Wood-Gooden, Kimberly. *Coping with Family Stress*. New York: Rosen Publishing Group, 1989.

PHYSICAL AND SEXUAL ABUSE

Bode, J. *The Voices of Rape*. New York: Dell, 1990.

Burgess, A.W. *Rape: Victims of Crisis*. Bowie, MD: Robert J. Brady Co., 1984.

———. *The Sexual Victimization of Adolescents*. Rockville MD: National Institute of Mental Health, 1985.

Cooney, Judith. *Coping with Sexual Abuse*, rev.ed. New York: Rosen Publishing Group, 1991.

Grubman-Black, S. *Broken Boys/Mending Men: Recovering from Childhood Sexual Abuse*, rev.ed. New York: Ballantine (Ivy), 1992.

Miller, Deborah A., and Kelly, Pat. *Coping with Incest*. New York: Rosen Publishing Group, 1992.

Parrott, Andrea. *Coping with Date Rape and Acquaintance Rape*, rev.ed. New York: Rosen Publishing Group, 1993.

SCHIZOPHRENIA

Korpell, H.S. *How You Can Help: A Guide for Families of Psychiatric Hospital Patients*. Washington DC: American Psychiatric Press, 1984.

Menninger, W.W., and Hannah, G. *The Chronic Mental Patient*. Washington DC: American Psychiatric Press, 1987.

SELF-CONCEPT, SELF-ESTEEM, BODY IMAGE

Bowen-Woodward, Kathy. *Coping with Negative Body Image.* New York: Rosen Publishing Group, 1989.

Cohen, Shari. *Coping with Failure.* New York: Rosen Publishing Group, 1988.

Hill, Margaret. *Coping with Family Expectations.* New York: Rosen Publishing Group, 1990.

Hislop, Julia. *Coping with Rejection.* New York: Rosen Publishing Group, 1991.

Ignoffo, Matthew. *Coping with Your Inner Critic.* New York: Rosen Publishing Group, 1990.

McFarland, Rhoda. *Coping with Self-Esteem*, rev.ed. New York: Rosen Publishing Group, 1993.

SEXUALITY

Cohen, S., and Cohen, D. *When Someone You Know Is Gay.* New York: Dell, 1989.

Miller, Deborah A., and Waigandt, Alex. *Coping with Your Sexual Orientation.* New York: Rosen Publishing Group, 1990.

Pomeroy, W.B. *Boys and Sex.* New York: Dell, 1991.

———. *Girls and Sex.* New York: Dell, 1991.

SUICIDE

Klagsbrun, F. *Too Young to Die: Youth and Suicide.* New York: Pocket Books, 1984.

Klerman, G.I. *Suicide and Depression Among Adolescents and Young Adults.* Washington DC: American Psychiatric Press, Inc., 1986.

Rue, N.N. *Coping with Suicide*, rev.ed. New York: Rosen Publishing Group, 1990.

RUNAWAYS

Connors, Patrieia, and Perrucci, Dorianna. *Runaways: Coping at Home and on the Street.* New York: Rosen Publishing Group, 1989.

Index

relationships, 19
  exploration of, 53
  self-quiz on, 11–12
  skills in, 65
  with therapist, 106–107
  understanding, 55
repression, 17, 111
resistance, to therapy, 18–21,
  22–31, 25–26, 64, 110–
  115
restructuring, cognitive, 60–61
Ritalin (methylphenidate), 148–
  149
role-playing, 39
Rorschach test, 172–173

S
schizophrenia, 74
school
  failure in, 36, 38
  self-quiz on, 10, 11
selective serotonin reuptake
  inhibitor (SSRI), 145
self-confidence, 28
self-esteem, 148
self-medication, 160–161
self-quizzes, 10–17, 101–102
sexual intimacy, 91–92
short-term psychotherapy, 64
siblings, talking to, 43–44
side effects, 145, 147, 152, 153,
  155–156
social skills, 59
social worker, 65, 72, 75, 76,
  154
  fees of, 120–121
Stanford Binet test, 178
Stelazine (trifluoperazine), 153
stimulant (Ritalin/

methylphenidate), 148, 149
suicide, 29, 134–135, 143

T
teacher, help from, 3, 17, 25,
  39, 40, 46, 48, 164
Tegretol (carbamazepine), 153
testing, 162–185
  individual, 176–180
  interpreting results of, 171–
  172, 179–180
  learning disabilities, 180–183
  mental, 175–180
  psychological, 50, 72, 74,
  144, 163, 164–167
Thematic Apperception Test
  (TAT), 173
therapies, differences in, 52-60
therapist
  changing, 89–90
  discussing money with, 118–
  119
  evaluating, 87–98, 105–106
  feelings about, 105–106
  finding, 81–86
  as guide, 23, 55
  not liking, 19
  in private practice, 119–121
  talking to parents, 36, 100–
  101
therapy
  court-ordered, 136–137
  family, 65–70
  group, 64–65
  individual, 63–64
  long-term, 54
  maintaining boundaries in,
  91–92
  need for, 9–21

procedures in, 99–115
process of, 108–115
terminating, 92–98
Thorazine (chlorpromazine), 153
Tofranil (imipramine), 145
training, psychotherapists', 72–
    78, 88
tranquilizer, major, 153–154
tricyclics, 145
trust
  loss of, 55
  of therapist, 107, 128

U
understanding
  gaining, 5

lack of, 36
seeking, 50–51, 54

V
Valium, 139
vocational aptitude test, 74,
    183–184

W
Wechsler Scales, 177–178

X
Xanax (alprazolam), 147

Z
Zoloft (setraline), 152